GCSE AQA
Biology
The Workbook

This book is for anyone doing **GCSE AQA Biology**.

It's full of **tricky questions**... each one designed to make you **sweat** — because that's the only way you'll get any **better**.

There are questions to see **what facts** you know. There are questions to see how well you can **apply those facts**. And there are questions to see what you know about **how science works**.

It's also got some daft bits in to try and make the whole experience at least vaguely entertaining for you.

What CGP is all about

Our sole aim here at CGP is to produce the highest quality books — carefully written, immaculately presented and dangerously close to being funny.

Then we work our socks off to get them out to you — at the cheapest possible prices.

Contents

The Nervous System

Q6 Some parts of the body are known as the CNS.

a) What do the letters **CNS** stand for? ....

b) Name the two main parts of the CNS.

1. .... 2. ....

c) What type of neurone:

i) carries information to the CNS? ....

ii) carries instructions from the CNS? ....

Q7 John and Marc investigated how **sensitive** different parts of the body are to **pressure**.
They stuck two pins in a cork 0.5 cm apart. The pins were placed on different parts of the body.
Ten pupils took part — they were blindfolded and reported "yes" or "no" to feeling both points.
The results of the experiment are shown in the table.

Area of the body tested	Number of pupils reporting 'yes'
Sole of foot	2
Knee	3
Fingertip	10
Back of hand	5
Lip	9

a) Which part of the body do the results suggest is:

i) most sensitive? .... **ii)** least sensitive ....

b) From the results above, which part of the body do you think
contains the **most pressure receptors**? Explain your answer.

....

....

c) John and Marc took it in turns to test the pupils. Their teacher suggested that if only one of
the boys had done all the testing, the experiment would have been fairer. Explain why.

....

....

d) Each pupil was tested once. Suggest how you might make the test more accurate.

....

....

Reflexes

Q1   Circle the correct answer to complete each of the following sentences.

a)   Reflexes happen more **quickly** / **slowly** than considered responses.

b)   The **vertebrae** / **spinal cord** can coordinate a reflex response.

c)   The main purpose of a reflex is to **protect** / **display** the body.

d)   Reflexes happen **with** / **without** you thinking about them.

e)   A synapse is a connection between two **effectors** / **neurones**.

Q2   Look carefully at the diagrams showing two different eyes below.

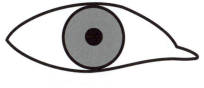

Eye A

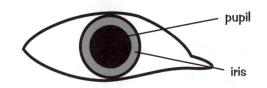

Eye B

pupil

iris

a)   Describe the difference you can see in the appearance of the two eyes.

....

....

b)   Which diagram do you think shows an eye in bright light? Explain your answer.

....

....

....

c)   Is the response illustrated by the diagrams above a considered response or a reflex response?

....

d)   Explain why it is an advantage to have this type of response controlling the action of the eye.

....

....

....

Reflexes

Q3 Why is a **reflex** reaction faster than a **voluntary** reaction?

Think about where the impulse has to go to.

....

....

Q4 Explain what a **reflex arc** is.

....

....

Q5 When you touch something hot with a finger you **automatically** pull the finger away. The diagram shows some parts of the nervous system involved in this **reflex action**.

receptor in skin

X

W

Y

muscle

Z

spinal cord

a) What type of neurone is:

i) neurone **X**? ....

ii) neurone **Y**? ....

iii) neurone **Z**? ....

b) In what form is the information carried:

i) along neurone **X**?

....

ii) from neurone **X** to neurone **Y**?

....

c) Complete the sentence.

In this reflex action the muscle acts as the ....

d) i) What are the gaps marked **W** on the diagram called? ....

ii) Explain how the impulse get across these gaps.

....

....

....

Top Tips: Reflexes are really fast — that's the whole point of them. And the fewer synapses the signals have to cross, the faster the reaction. Doctors test people's reflexes by tapping below their knees to make their legs jerk. This reflex takes less than 50 milliseconds as only two synapses are involved.

Hormones

Q1   Complete the passage below about **hormones**.

> Hormones are .... messengers. They are produced in
> .... and released into the ....
> They are carried all around the body, but only affect certain .... cells.

Q2   What is the '**fight or flight**' hormone? Why is it known in this way?

....

....

Q3   Fit the answers to the clues into the grid.

  a)   Gland that produces insulin

  b)   Hormone produced by the pituitary

  c)   Insulin controls the level of this in the blood

  d)   Transports hormones around the body

  e)   Hormone produced by the testes

Q4   Describe the major differences between responses brought
about by **hormones** and those due to the **nervous system**.

....

....

....

Q5   ADH is a hormone which causes the kidneys to remove less water from the blood.

  a)   Name gland X.   ....

  b)   Suggest what triggers gland X to produce ADH.

....

....

gland **X**
produces ADH   brain

blood
returns
to brain

ADH
transported
in blood

kidney

The Menstrual Cycle

Q1   FSH has two functions in the menstrual cycle.

a)   What are these functions?

1. ....

2. ....

b)   What effect does oestrogen have on the production of FSH?

....

Q2   Answer the following questions about **LH**.

a)   What does LH stand for?

....

b)   What causes LH to be released?

....

c)   When does the LH cause the release of an egg from the ovary?

....

Q3   There are three main **hormones** involved in the menstrual cycle.

a)   Complete the table to show **where** in the body each hormone is produced.

HORMONE	WHERE IT IS PRODUCED
FSH	
oestrogen	
LH	

b)   Give two effects that oestrogen has in the body of an adult woman.

1. ....

2. ....

Top Tips: Sometimes, it's haaard to be... a womaaan... Or a man for that matter, if you're trying to learn about the menstrual cycle. This isn't really a topic where your natural intelligence and deep understanding of science can shine through much — you've just got to get your head down and learn the four stages and what each hormone does. Sorry.

The Menstrual Cycle

Q4 These diagrams show some events in the **menstrual cycle**. Put the events in the order they happen in the menstrual cycle by writing numbers in the boxes, then describe each event **briefly**.

Don't forget, the cycle begins with the first day of a period.

☐ ....

....

☐ ....

....

☐ ....

....

Don't forget, 'uterus' is just the biological word for the 'womb'.

Q5 An **egg** is usually released on day 14 of the menstrual cycle.

a) Why does the uterus wall become thick and spongy before the egg is released?

....

....

b) Explain why there are only a few days in each menstrual cycle when fertilisation can take place.

....

....

c) What happens in the uterus if the egg is not fertilised?

....

Controlling Fertility

Q1 Hormones can be used to **increase fertility**.

a) Name the hormone that is often given to women who are not releasing any eggs.

....

b) The passage below explains how this hormone works.
Use the words in the box to fill in the gaps. Each word should be used once.

pituitary gland	LH	egg	FSH	ovary	oestrogen

.... stimulates the ovaries to produce .... ,

which stimulates the .... to produce ....

This stimulates the .... to release an ....

Q2 Using hormones to increase or reduce fertility in women has some **disadvantages**.
Complete the table below to show some of the disadvantages of taking hormones.

Use	Possible disadvantages
Reducing fertility	1. ....
	2. ....
Increasing fertility	1. ....
	2. ....

Q3 **The pill** is an **oral contraceptive** that contains oestrogen. Explain how it is used to reduce fertility.

....

....

Q4 **In vitro fertilisation** can help couples to have children.

a) Explain how **in vitro fertilisation** works.

....

....

....

b) Discuss the advantages and disadvantages of in vitro fertilisation.

....

....

....

Homeostasis

Q1 Define **homeostasis**.

....

....

Q2 The human body is usually maintained at a temperature of about **37 ºC**.

a) Why do humans suffer ill effects if their body temperature varies too much from this temperature?

....

....

b) Which part of your body monitors your body temperature to ensure that it is kept constant?

....

c) How does your body cool down when it is too hot?

....

Q3 The graph shows the **blood sugar levels** of a healthy person over a period of 5 hours.

a) What might have caused the drop in blood sugar level at point A?

....

b) The blood sugar level rose quickly at point B. What could have caused this increase in sugar level?

....

c) **i)** Which hormone caused the blood sugar to return to normal at point C?

....

ii) Where in the body is this hormone produced? Underline the correct answer below.

The pituitary gland　　　　　　　　**The kidneys**

The muscles　　　　　　　　　　**The pancreas**

Homeostasis

Q4   Choose the correct words to complete the paragraph below.

On a **cold** / **hot** day or when you're exercising, you **sweat a lot** / **don't sweat much**, so

you will produce **more** / **less** urine. The urine will be a **pale** / **dark** colour as it contains

less / **more** water than usual. We say that the urine is more **concentrated** / **dilute** than usual.

Q5   Ronald eats a meal that is very high in **salt**. Which of the answers below explain correctly how Ronald's body gets rid of this excess salt? Tick one or more boxes.

☐	Ronald's liver removes salt from his blood.
☐	Ronald loses salt in his sweat.
☐	Ronald's kidneys remove salt from his blood.
☐	Ronald's saliva becomes more salty, and the salt is lost when he breathes.
☐	Ronald gets rid of salt in his urine.

Q6   The Big Brother contestants are getting on my nerves, so I put each of them on a treadmill and turn the setting to high (just to keep them quiet for a bit).

Will the contestants lose **more** or **less** water from the following body parts than they would if they sat still? Explain your answers.

a) Skin ....

....

b) Lungs ....

....

c) Kidneys ....

....

Q7   Mrs Finnegan had the **concentration of ions** in her urine measured on two days.

Date	6th December	20th July
Average air temperature	8 °C	24 °C
Ion concentration in urine	1.5 mg/cm³	2.1 mg/cm³

Assuming Mrs Finnegan always eats exactly the same food every day, suggest a reason for the different ion concentrations in her urine.

....

....

Diet and Exercise

Q1   The bar chart shows the proportions of each **food group** that make up three different foods.

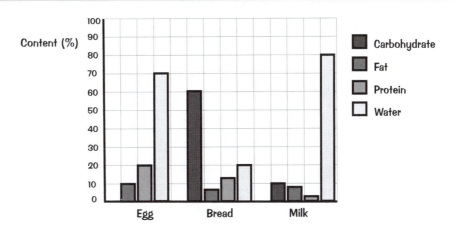

a)   Which food contains the highest proportion of fat? ....

b)   What is the difference between the amount of carbohydrate in 50 g of bread and the amount of carbohydrate in 50 g of milk? Give your answer in grams and show your working out.

....

....

The % in the bar chart is like the no. of grams you'd have in 100 g of the food.

c)   For my lunch I have scrambled eggs on toast and a glass of milk. Suggest another food I could have to make this a more balanced meal. Explain your answer.

....

....

Q2   Different people need to eat **different amounts** of food because they have different energy requirements.

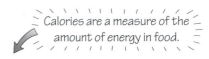

Calories are a measure of the amount of energy in food.

a)   It is recommended that the average woman eats about 2000 Calories per day, while the average man should eat about 2500 Calories. Explain why there is a difference.

....

....

b)   Cyclists riding in the Tour de France bike race need to eat about 6000 Calories per day during the race. This is more than twice what the average man requires. Explain why.

....

....

Top Tips: Mmm, what I couldn't do with 6000 Calories per day... Anyway, remember that everyone needs a balanced diet, but not everyone needs to eat exactly the same stuff. The amount you need depends on your metabolic rate and how much exercise you do — more on this on the next page.

Diet and Exercise

Q3 Answer the following questions about **metabolism**.

a) What is meant by 'metabolic rate'?

....

....

b) What effect does being overweight have on your metabolic rate? Explain your answer.

....

....

c) How would taking up regular exercise affect your resting metabolic rate? Explain your answer.

....

....

Q4 Explain why you need less energy from your diet if you live in a hot climate.

....

....

Q5 Complete the following sentences to show the functions in the body of different food groups.

a) Protein is needed for .... and ....

b) Carbohydrates provide much of your ....

c) Fats are needed to .... and for ....

d) Fibre keeps your .... working smoothly.

e) Vitamins and minerals are needed in .... amounts to stay healthy.

Q6 How can a person be both 'fit' and **malnourished**?

....

....

Weight Problems

Q1 Lack of food is often a problem in developing countries.

a) Write down two common effects of malnutrition.

....

b) Children tend to be particularly badly affected when there is a shortage of food. Suggest why.

....

Q2 Explain why it can be difficult for researchers to collect **accurate data** on:

a) malnutrition and starvation. ....

....

....

b) obesity. ....

....

....

Q3 Fifty men and fifty women were asked whether they thought they were **obese**.
Each was then given a medical examination to **check** whether they were actually obese.

	Thought they were obese	Actually obese
No. of women	9	16
No. of men	5	11

a) What percentage of women in this survey were obese? ....

b) What are the most common causes of obesity in developed countries?

....

c) Is an obesity study based on data from questionnaires likely to be accurate?
Explain your answer.

....

....

d) Underline any health problems in the list below that have been linked to obesity.

heart disease   **hepatitis**   **influenza**   **cancers**   **scurvy**   **diabetes**

Q4 Explain how high levels of obesity could cause **economic problems** in a country like the UK.

....

....

14

Cholesterol and Salt

Q1 There are several **risk factors** for heart disease.

  a) What is meant by a 'risk factor' for heart disease?

  ....

  b) How does a high level of salt in your diet affect your body?

  ....

Q2 It is recommended that adults should eat no more than **6 g** of salt each day.

  a) Your friend tells you that there is no way that she can be eating
       too much salt as she never sprinkles any on her food. Is she right?

  ....

  ....

  b) The salt in food is usually listed as sodium in the nutritional information on the label.
       You can work out the amount of salt using the formula: **salt = sodium × 2.5**

       It says there is **0.5 g of sodium per serving** of soup. How much salt is this?

  ....

  ....

Q3 This question is about **lipoproteins**.

  a) What are lipoproteins?

  ....

  b) Name the two types of lipoproteins involved in the transport of cholesterol in the blood.

  ....

  c) Explain what is meant by 'bad cholesterol' and 'good cholesterol'.

  ....

  ....

  ....

Q4 Name the three main types of fat found in our diet and say how their **carbon chains** differ.

  ....

  ....

  ....

Cholesterol and Salt

Q5   In a minor **heart attack** the flow of blood in the heart muscle is reduced.

a)   Explain how too much cholesterol can lead to this type of heart attack.

....

....

b)   Which organ controls the level of cholesterol in the body?

....

Q6   The following table shows the **fat content** of two different butter substitute spreads.

TYPE OF FAT	PERCENTAGE IN SPREAD A	PERCENTAGE IN SPREAD B
Saturated	10	50
Monounsaturated	35	31
Polyunsaturated	54	15
Trans fatty acids	1	4

a)   Complete the pie charts to show this information.

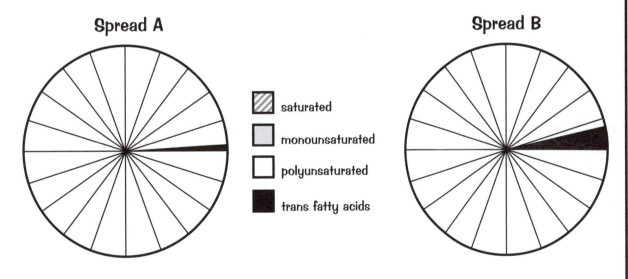

b)   The packaging of one of the spreads says it is 'proven to reduce cholesterol levels'. Which spread do you think this is? Explain your answer.

....

....

Top Tips: Mmm, I just fancy a plate of chips now... It's a bit depressing, all this 'risk factor', 'bad cholesterol' talk, isn't it? But don't be scared — just about everything is bad for you if you do it too much. Even chips are OK in moderation — just don't have them every day.

Drugs

Q1 a) What does the term 'drug' mean?

....

b) What does it mean if you are **addicted** to a drug?

....

....

Q2 Write numbers in the boxes below to show the correct **order** in which drugs are tested.

☐ **Drug is tested on human tissue.**

☐ **Computer models simulate a response to the drug.**

☐ **Human volunteers are used to test the drug.**

☐ **Drug is tested on live animals.**

Q3 Before drugs are made freely available, **clinical trials** must be performed.

a) What is a 'clinical trial'?

....

b) Give two reasons why clinical trials have to be done before drugs are made freely available.

....

....

c) Explain why clinical trials can't be done on human tissue samples only.

....

....

Q4 **Thalidomide** is a drug that was developed in the 1950s.

a) What was this drug originally developed for?

....

b) Thalidomide was not fully tested. What effect did it have when given to pregnant women?

....

....

c) Why has this drug been reintroduced recently?

....

Q5 Outline the arguments for and against using **live animals** for testing new drugs.

....

....

....

Alcohol and Tobacco

Q1 In the UK, the legal limit for alcohol in the blood when driving is **80 mg per 100 cm³**. The table shows the number of 'units' of alcohol in different drinks. One **unit** increases the blood alcohol level by over **20 mg per 100 cm³** in most people.

DRINK	ALCOHOL UNITS
1 pint of strong lager	3
1 pint of beer	2
1 single measure of whisky	1

a) Bill drinks two pints of strong lager. How many units of alcohol has he had? ....

b) Is Bill's blood alcohol level likely to mean that he cannot legally drive? Explain your answer.

....

....

Assume he drank the cans fairly quickly.

c) Explain why it can be dangerous to drive a car after drinking alcohol.

....

Q2 a) Alcohol can cause **dehydration**. What effect does this have on the brain?

....

b) Which other organ is often damaged by excessive alcohol intake? ....

Q3 The graph shows how the number of **smokers** aged between 35 and 54 in the UK has changed since 1950.

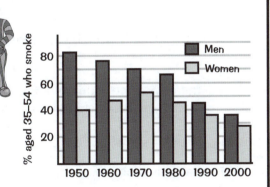

a) Describe the main trends you can see in this graph.

....

....

....

....

b) Why are smokers more likely to suffer from:

i) chest infections ....

....

ii) cancers ....

Q4 a) Why do alcohol and smoking have a **bigger impact** than illegal drugs in the UK?

....

b) Give two ways in which misuse of alcohol and smoking **negatively** affect the **economy** in the UK.

....

....

Investigating Drugs

Q1 Smoking is now known to be dangerous and many people try to give up. People often find this **difficult** so there are products and methods to help them. These include **hypnosis**, **acupuncture** and **nicotine replacement** using patches or gums.

a) Why is it hard to give up smoking?

....

b) Which of the methods listed above is supported most by scientific evidence?

....

c) Explain how nicotine gum may help someone to give up.

....

....

Q2 Decide which of these statements are **facts** and which are **opinions**. Write '**F**' for fact or '**O**' for opinion in each box.

Crack cocaine is highly addictive.

Using cannabis relaxes you.

Only people with addictive personalities become addicts.

Soft drugs are safe to use.

Heroin can relieve pain.

Q3 There are three main opinions about the **link** between cannabis and hard drugs. Explain the idea behind each of the following:

a) Stepping stone: ....

b) Gateway drug: ....

c) Genetics: ....

Q4 In the early 20th century, the number of people developing **lung cancer** was increasing. At the same time it was noted that more people were **smoking**.

a) Give **three** possible explanations for the correlation between lung cancer and smoking.

1. ....

2. ....

3. ....

b) Which of your explanations do you think cigarette manufacturers favoured? Explain your answer.

....

....

Investigating Drugs

Q5   Read the article below and answer the questions that follow.

In the UK, all illegal drugs belong to one of three classes — A, B or C — depending on how harmful they are. The punishments for possessing (or dealing) class A drugs are more severe than for class C drugs.

In January 2004, cannabis was 'reclassified' as a class C drug. Previously, it had been in class B, along with amphetamines like 'speed'. The Government decided to 'downgrade' cannabis because most evidence showed that it was less harmful than the other class B drugs.

There's still a lot of debate about how harmful cannabis is, though. Many people are worried that cannabis is linked to mental illnesses like depression and schizophrenia.

 In one study, scientists monitored the mental health of about 1600 teenagers at 44 different schools in Australia, over a seven-year period.

They found that girls who used cannabis every day were five times more likely to suffer from depression by the age of 20. Those who used cannabis less frequently (but at least once a week) were twice as likely to suffer from depression as non-users.

Another team of scientists studied a group of older men in Sweden. Their study involved 50 000 men who did their compulsory military service between 1969 and 1970. When they began military service (aged 18–20), these men all gave details about how often they used cannabis (and other drugs). The researchers then examined the men's medical records from 1970 to 1996, to see how many of them suffered from schizophrenia in later life. They found that the more frequently a person used cannabis, the more likely they were to develop schizophrenia.

Remember that the independent variable is the one that is changed, and the dependent variable is the one that is measured.

a)   The following questions are about the **Swedish** study.

i) What were the dependent and independent variables in this study?

Dependent variable: ....

Independent variable: ....

ii) Drug use was measured by asking the men how often they used drugs. What is the main problem with this kind of '**self-reporting**'?

....

....

b)   Fill in the information below about the **Australian** study.

Sample size: ....

Time period covered: ....

Independent variable: ....

Dependent variable: ....

Investigating Drugs

c) **i)** Write 'true' or 'false' next to each of the statements below.

 A Cannabis was legalised in 2004. ....

 B Punishments for dealing class A drugs are harsher than for dealing class C drugs. ....

 C Amphetamines are class C drugs. ....

 D Most evidence suggests that cannabis is more harmful than class A drugs. ....

 ii) Write correct versions of the statements above that are **false**.

 ....

 ....

 ....

d) The **Australian** study looked at cannabis use amongst teenage girls.

 i) Complete the bar chart of the results.

 Read over the passage again if you're not sure. Remember, the bar chart gives you the level for those girls who never used cannabis.

 ii) What link is suggested by this study?

 ....

 ....

 ....

Number of girls suffering from depression after different frequencies of cannabis use

Number of girls suffering from depression

daily   at least   never
         weekly

Frequency of cannabis use

 iii) Do these results **prove** that cannabis use causes depression? Explain your answer.

 ....

 ....

 ....

e) Which of the two studies do you think provides the most **reliable** results, and why?

 ....

 ....

 ....

Top Tips: So, after all that time, effort and money, the answer is ...erm, we dunno. Maybe it causes mental health problems, and then again, maybe it doesn't. That's science for you. There could be **another factor** that makes people more likely to take drugs **and** more likely to become mentally ill.

Health Claims

Q1 Scientists are still **not sure** whether there is a link between using cannabis and developing mental health problems, despite the fact that lots of studies have been carried out. Explain why this is.

....

....

Q2 Two reports on **low-fat foods** were published on one day. **Report A** appeared in a tabloid paper. It said that the manufacturers of 'Crunchie Bites' have shown that the latest girl band, Kandyfloss, lost weight using their product. **Report B** appeared in a journal and reported how 6000 volunteers lost weight during a trial of an experimental medicine.

Which of these reports is likely to be the most reliable and why?

....

....

Q3 Three **weight loss methods** appeared in the headlines last week.

① **Hollywood star swears carrot soup aids weight loss**

② **Survey of 10 000 dieters shows it's exercise that counts**

③ **Atkins works! 5000 in study lose weight... but what about their health?**

a) Which of these headlines are more likely to refer to **scientific studies**? Explain your answer.

....

....

b) Why might following the latest celebrity diet not always help you lose weight?

....

....

Q4 A drug trial involved 6000 patients with **high cholesterol levels**. 3000 patients were given **statins**, and 3000 were not. Both were advised to make lifestyle changes to lower their cholesterol. The decrease in their cholesterol levels compared to their levels at the start is shown on the graph.

a) Why was the group without statin included? ....

....

b) Suggest a conclusion that can be drawn from these results. ....

....

Fighting Disease

Q1 Fill in the gaps in the passage below using the words in the box.

cells	bursts	celled	DNA	damaging	toxins	damage	copies

Bacteria are single-............................... organisms which can multiply rapidly. Some can

make you ill by .... your body cells or producing ....

Viruses are tiny particles — they are not .... They are often made up of

a coat of protein and a strand of .... Viruses replicate by fooling body cells

into making .... of them. The cell then .... and releases

the new virus. This cell .... makes you feel ill.

Q2 If a person has an organ transplant, they may have to take drugs to **suppress** their immune system and stop the organ being **rejected**. Why is it important that these people **avoid infection**?

....

....

Q3 **White blood cells** protect the body from infection.

a) Give **three** ways that they do this.

....

....

....

b) How do white blood cells recognise particular types of pathogen?

....

c) Explain what **natural immunity** is.

....

....

....

d) How does the body try to protect itself from infection through cuts?

....

....

Biology 1a — Human Biology

Fighting Disease

Q4   Define these terms.

a)   pathogen: ....

b)   immunisation: ....

c)   antigens: ....

d)   booster: ....

Q5   A new medicine called 'Killcold' contains **painkillers** and **decongestants**.

a)   Explain why its name isn't strictly accurate.

....

....

b)   Why don't doctors give antibiotics for colds?

....

....

c)   Why is it more difficult to develop drugs to destroy viruses than it is to develop drugs to kill bacteria?

Think about where in the body viruses like to hang out so that they can replicate themselves.

....

....

Q6   John gets injected with the **rubella vaccine** but James doesn't. Soon afterwards both boys are exposed to the rubella virus. Explain why James gets ill but John **doesn't**.

....

....

....

Q7   Jay is given **antibiotics** for an infection. Soon he feels better, so he doesn't finish the full course of antibiotics. How may this lead to the development of **antibiotic-resistant strains** of bacteria?

....

....

....

Top Tips: Pathogens are all nasty little blighters that make you ill if they manage to get inside you. Bacteria and viruses are both pathogens but they have totally different structures and methods of attack — make sure you know the differences. And remember — antibiotics kill bacteria, not viruses.

24

Treating Disease — Past and Future

Q1 Answer the questions below about **immunisation**.

a) Describe how immunisations have changed the pattern of disease in the UK.

....

....

b) Name a disease that has been **eradicated** worldwide because of immunisation programmes.

....

c) Describe **two** problems that occasionally occur with vaccines.

....

....

Q2 The MMR vaccine protects against measles, mumps and rubella. There is a small risk that children will suffer serious side effects to the vaccine such as meningitis or convulsions. However, the Government recommends that **all** children are given the MMR vaccine. Explain why this is.

....

....

....

Q3 Ignaz Semmelweiss worked in a hospital in Vienna in the 1840s. The graph shows the percentage of women dying after childbirth, before and after a **change** that he made.

a) What was the change and why did it help?

....

....

....

b) After Semmelweiss left, the doctors went back to their old ways. Why do you think this was?

....

....

Biology 1a — Human Biology

Treating Disease — Past and Future

Q4 The graph shows the number of people catching **measles**, and the number being **immunised** against it in the UK.

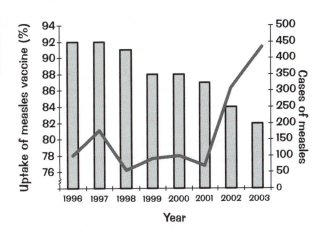

☐ Uptake of measles vaccine (%)

── Cases of measles

*Number of cases of measles includes those confirmed by testing serum & by oral fluid.

a) What happened to the number of people catching measles as the number being immunised decreased over the time period shown on the graph?

....

b) The graph appears to show a **threshold level** of immunisation. When the percentage of people being immunised falls **below** this threshold level, the number of measles cases starts increasing. What is this threshold level?

....

c) The **more** people there are in the population that **have** been immunised against measles, the **less likely** you are to catch it, even if you yourself have **not** been immunised. Explain why.

....

....

Q5 Some bacteria and viruses **evolve quickly**.

a) Why is rapid **bacterial** evolution such a threat to human health?

....

....

b) It can be difficult to find an effective **vaccine** against diseases caused by pathogens that evolve rapidly. Explain why.

....

....

....

Top Tips:

Of course, Darwin was right when he said that evolution happens gradually over many generations. The trouble is, with bacteria and viruses, a whole generation can take about ten minutes. Hmmm.

Mixed Questions — Biology 1a

Q1   The diagram shows a runner waiting to start a race in the Olympic Games.

   a)   Give one sense organ that the athlete is relying on at the start of the race, and state the type of receptors it uses.

   ....

   b)   When the athlete starts the race, information will travel around his body via neurones.
   i)   What is the difference between motor neurones and sensory neurones?

   ....

   ii)   Explain how a nerve signal passes from one neurone to the next.

   ....

   ....

   c)   Some information is sent around the body using hormones rather than nervous impulses.

   i)   How do hormones travel around the body?

   ....

   ii)   Describe **three** differences in the way nerves and hormones work in the body.

   ....

   ....

   ....

Q2   The diagram represents the **menstrual cycle** in a particular woman.

   a)   What is the length of the complete menstrual cycle shown?
   .... days.

   b)   What happens on day 16 of this woman's cycle?

   ....

   c)   Oestrogen is one of the main hormones that control the menstrual cycle.
   What other role does oestrogen have in the female body?

   ....

   d)   Explain how the oestrogen in the contraceptive pill prevents pregnancy.

   ....

   ....

Mixed Questions — Biology 1a

Q3 a) Complete the passage below by choosing the correct words to fill in the gaps.

saturated	salt	HDL	LDL	hypertension	polyunsaturated	scurvy	liver

The amount of cholesterol in the blood is controlled by the ....
Cholesterol is transported around the body by two kinds of lipoprotein. One is known as 'good cholesterol' or .... The other form is ...., and is sometimes called 'bad cholesterol'. Eating more .... fats can improve the balance between good and bad cholesterol.

b) A high 'bad' cholesterol level puts you at risk of heart disease.
Give two factors linked to **diet** that also affect your chances of getting heart disease.

....

Q4 a) Circle the best word or phrase from each pair to complete the sentences below.

i) **Carbohydrates / Vitamins** are needed in tiny amounts to keep you healthy.

ii) Obesity tends to be a problem in **developed / developing** countries.

iii) An overweight person usually has a **higher / lower** metabolic rate than an average person.

iv) A farmer is likely to need a lot **more / less** energy than someone working in a call centre.

v) Carbohydrates are broken down into sugars to provide **energy / materials to build new cells**.

b) Water is a vital part of our diet and the body's water level is controlled by homeostasis.

i) Name three ways that water is lost from the body.

....

ii) Explain why the amount of urine that people produce can depend on the air temperature.

....

....

Q5 Scientists spend a lot of time **researching** new diets and drugs.

a) Why are drugs tested on animals before they are used in clinical trials?

....

b) List three factors that can give you an indication of how reliable a scientific report is.

....

....

Mixed Questions — Biology 1a

Q6 Tick the boxes below that are next to **true** statements.

It is now widely accepted that smoking increases the risk of lung cancer.

Alcohol doesn't tend to cause serious problems because it is legal.

It is now widely accepted that using cannabis increases the risk of mental health problems.

Until more scientific evidence is available, scientists can't be sure that smoking is harmful.

Some studies have found a link between cannabis use and mental health problems.

It has been proven that the desire to take cannabis and other drugs is genetic.

Q7 Gavin and Van carried out an experiment at school to investigate the effectiveness of six different **antibiotics** (1–6). They spread some bacteria onto a sterile agar plate. They then placed discs of filter paper, impregnated with the six different antibiotics, onto the bacterial culture.

a) Define the term "antibiotic".

....

b) Explain what has happened in the "clear zone" labelled on the diagram.

....

c) Which of the antibiotics (1–6) was the most effective against these bacteria? ....

d) Would these antibiotics also work against the flu? Explain your answer.

....

e) Why do doctors prescribe antibiotics as infrequently as possible?

....

....

f) Fortunately, many people with infections don't need antibiotics because their bodies have ways of dealing with pathogens. Explain how some white blood cells use antibodies to kill bacteria.

....

....

g) Why are people vaccinated against diseases such as mumps even though their white blood cells are able to fight the pathogens?

....

Adapt and Survive

Q1 Pictures of a **polar bear** and a small rodent called a **kangaroo rat** are shown below.

Diagrams are
not to scale.

a) Which of these animals do you think has the smallest body surface area? ....

b) Which animal has the smallest body
surface area **compared to its volume**? ....

*This is a tricky one. Remember, long,
thin shapes have a big surface area
compared to their volume.*

c) Explain how this animal's **shape** helps to reduce its
body surface area compared to its volume.

....

d) Does having a **smaller** body surface area compared to volume mean that more or less **heat** can be
lost from an animal's body?

....

e) The kangaroo rat lives in hot desert regions. Would you expect its body surface area compared to
volume to be bigger or smaller than the polar bear's? Explain why.

....

....

....

Q2 The picture shows a **cactus** plant.

a) Where are cactus plants usually found? Underline the correct answer below.

In Arctic regions   **In the desert**   **In the mountains**   **Near the sea**

b) Explain how each of the following parts of the cactus help it to survive in its normal habitat.

i) Spines ....

....

ii) Stem ....

....

iii) Roots ....

....

Adapt and Survive

Q3 Complete the passage using the words given. Each can be used more than once or not at all.

| heat | concentrated | sweat | water | large | offspring | small | night | dilute |

Mammals living in deserts need to conserve .... They make ....

amounts of very .... urine. They also produce very little ....

They keep cool in other ways, e.g. by only coming out at ....

Q4 The picture shows two different types of fox.

Fox A   Fox B

a) State two differences in the appearance of the foxes.

1. ....

2. ....

b) Identify which fox lives in a cold Arctic region and which lives in a desert.

i) Fox A ....   **ii)** Fox B ....

c) Explain how the features you described in part a) help each fox to survive in its natural habitat.

1. ....

....

2. ....

....

Q5 Hayley measured some cubes to find out their surface area to volume ratio. Her results are shown in the table.

a) Calculate the **surface area : volume ratio** for each cube and write your answers in the table. *Just divide the surface area by the volume.*

Length of cube side (cm)	Surface area of cube (cm²)	Volume of cube (cm²)	Surface area: volume ratio
2	24	8	
4	96	64	
6	216	216	
8	384	512	
10	600	1000	

b) As the cube size becomes larger, what happens to the value of the **surface area : volume ratio**?

....

c) Would you expect the smallest cube (length 2 cm) or the largest cube (length 10 cm) to lose heat more quickly? Explain your answer.

....

d) Use your answers above to explain why a mouse has a thick covering of fur.

....

....

Populations and Competition

Q1 Indicate whether each behaviour involves animals trying to compete (**C**) or acting as predators (**P**) by putting a cross in the correct column.

BEHAVIOUR	C	P
Stags grow antlers during the mating season		
A pack of wolves work together to kill a moose		
A magpie chases a sparrow away from a bird-table		
Spiders spin webs to trap flies		
Lions chase leopards and cheetahs from their territory		

Q2 **Algae** are tiny plants that are eaten by **fish**. The graph shows how the size of a population of algae in a pond varied throughout one year.

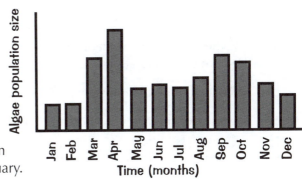

a) Suggest two conditions that may have changed in the pond to give more algae in April than in January.

....

b) The number of **fish** in the pond increased rapidly during one month of the year. Suggest which month this was. Explain your answer.

....

....

Q3 Jenny cultured some bacteria in a Petri dish. She counted the number of colonies (clumps of cells) at intervals as they spread across the dish. Her results are shown in the table.

Time (minutes)	No. of bacterial colonies
0	1
20	2
40	4
60	8
80	16
100	32
120	64

a) Suggest two things Jenny had to provide the bacteria with to allow them to grow.

1) .... 2) ....

b) Calculate the number of bacterial colonies you would expect to find after 3 hours.

....

Hint: look for a pattern in Jenny's results and continue it.

c) After 3 hours, Jenny found that the number of bacterial colonies stopped increasing. Suggest why this might be.

....

....

__Populations and Competition__

Q4   The table shows how the UK's barn owl population
has changed over a period of 20 years.

Year	No. of barn owl pairs (thousands)
1970	7
1980	4.5
1990	1.4

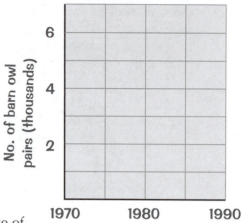

a)   Use the table to plot a graph showing the change in the size of
the barn owl population over time. Use the grid provided.

b)   Estimate the population size in 1985. ....

c)   Suggest **two** reasons why the barn owl population has decreased in recent years.

....

....

Q5   The graph shows how the size of a
population of **deer** and a population
of **wolves** living in the same area
changed over time.

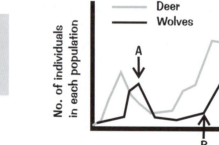

a)   Describe the pattern in the changing
sizes of these two populations.

....

....

b)   Explain why the two populations are connected in this way.

....

c)   At one point during the period covered by this graph, the wolves were affected by a disease.
Underline one of the options below to show when this was.

          At point A   **At point B**   **At point C**

d)   What effect did the disease have on the size of the **deer** population? Suggest why this happened.

....

....

Variation in Plants and Animals

Q1 Complete this passage by circling the **best** word or phrase from each highlighted pair.

> Usually, organisms of the same species **have differences / are identical**.
>
> This is partly because different organisms have different **genes / cells**, which
>
> they inherit from their parents. **Siblings / Identical twins** are exceptions to this.
>
> But even these usually have some different features, such as **hair style / eye colour**,
>
> and that is due to their **diet / environment**. The differences between individual
>
> organisms are known as **variation / inheritance**.

Q2 Helen and Stephanie are identical twins. Helen has dark hair and Stephanie is blonde.

   a) Do you think that these are Helen and Stephanie's natural hair colours? Explain your answer.

   ....

   ....

   b) Helen weighs 7 kg more than Stephanie. Say whether this is due to genes, environment or both, and explain your answer.

   ....

   ....

   c) Stephanie has a birthmark on her shoulder shaped like Wayne Rooney. Helen doesn't. Do you think birthmarks are caused by your genes? Explain why.

   ....

   ....

Q3 Mr O'Riley breeds racehorses. He breeds his best black racing stallion, Snowball, with his best black racing mare, Goldie.

   a) Why is there no guarantee that any foal born will be a champion racer?

   ....

   ....

   b) Will the colour of the newborn foal be due to genes or to environment?

   ....

Variation in Plants and Animals

Q4 The peppered moth is an insect that is often found on tree bark and is preyed on by birds. There are two varieties of peppered moth — a light form and a dark form. Until the 1850s, the light form was more common, but after then the dark form increased a lot, particularly near cities.

Moths on tree bark in
unpolluted area

Moths on tree bark in
polluted area

a) Why do you think the lighter variety of the peppered moth was more common originally?

....

Hint: Use
the diagrams
to help you.

....

b) In the 1850s, the Industrial Revolution began — there was rapid growth in heavy industries in Britain. Why do you think the number of dark moths increased after this time?

....

....

c) Do you think a difference in genes or in environment would cause a dark moth to suddenly appear in a population of light moths? ....

Q5 Nazneen grows three strawberry plants and three sunflowers.

a) Why do the strawberry plants look so different to the sunflower plants?

....

b) Sunflower plants reproduce by sexual reproduction. Why could Nazneen not expect her three sunflower plants to be exactly the same height?

....

....

c) Nazneen's strawberry plants were grown by asexual reproduction. However, her three strawberry plants are not all exactly the same height. Explain why this might be.

....

....

Genes, Chromosomes and DNA

Q1 Complete the passage using some of the words given below.

DNA	nucleus	genes	chromosomes	membrane	allele

Each cell of the body contains a structure called the ....

This structure contains strands of genetic information, packaged into ....

These strands are made of a chemical called ....

Sections of genetic material that control different characteristics are called ....

Q2 Write out these structures in order of size, **starting with the smallest**.

nucleus	gene	chromosome	cell

1. .... 2. .... 3. .... 4. ....

Q3 Which of the following is the correct definition of the term '**alleles**'? Underline your choice.

'Alleles' is the collective term for all the genes found on a pair of chromosomes.

'Alleles' are different forms of the same gene.

'Alleles' are identical organisms produced by asexual reproduction.

Q4 Only one of the following statements is true. Tick the correct one.

There are two chromosome 7s in a human nucleus, both from the person's mother. ☐

There are two chromosome 7s in a human nucleus, both from the person's father. ☐

There are two chromosome 7s in a human nucleus, one from each parent. ☐

There is only one chromosome 7 in a human nucleus. ☐

Q5 The human chromosome 15 contains a gene that is involved in controlling eye colour. How many chromosome 15s would you expect to find in each of the following cells?

a) A cell in the retina of the eye. ....

b) A muscle cell. ....

c) A sperm cell. ....

Top Tips:
First of all you need to know exactly what's meant by genes, alleles, DNA, chromosomes, etc.
And don't forget that virtually all organisms have two of each chromosome in their body cells.

Biology 1b — Evolution and Environment

Reproduction

Q1 Circle the correct words in each statement below to complete the sentences.

a) Sexual reproduction involves **one** / **two** individual(s).

b) The cells that are involved in asexual reproduction are called **parent cells** / **gametes**.

c) Asexual reproduction produces offspring with **identical** / **different** genes to the parent.

d) In sexual reproduction the sperm cell contains **the same number of** / **half as many** chromosomes as the **fertilised** egg.

e) **Asexual** / **Sexual** reproduction creates offspring with different characteristics to the parent(s).

Q2 Complete the following sentences.

a) Offspring that are identical to their parent are called ....

b) The male gamete is a ....

c) The process that occurs when two gametes fuse is ....

Q3 Lucy cut her hand, but a week later she noticed that the cut had almost disappeared. The skin covering it looked just the same as the skin on the rest of her hand. This happened by the same process as **asexual reproduction**.

a) Where did the new skin cells on Lucy's hand come from?

....

....

b) Suggest why the skin on Lucy's hand looked the same as it had before she had cut herself.

....

....

c) Suggest why it took a week for the cut to heal.

....

....

Q4 Explain how a human baby receives genes from both its father and its mother, but still only has 46 chromosomes in its cells.

....

....

....

Cloning

Q1 Joe has a herd of cows and he wants them all to have calves, but he **only** wants to breed from his champion bull and prize cow.

a) Name a method Joe could use to achieve this. ....

b) Describe the steps involved in this method in detail.

....

....

....

c) Which of the animals involved in this process will be genetically identical?

....

d) Give one disadvantage of this method.

....

....

Q2 a) Describe the process that was used to create **Dolly the sheep**.

....

....

....

b) Explain how this process could be adapted and used to help treat problems such as kidney disease.

....

....

Q3 a) Name the **two** methods commonly used by man to produce clones of plants.

....

b) Give **two** advantages and **one** disadvantage of cloning plants using methods like these.

Advantage 1: ....

Advantage 2: ....

Disadvantage: ....

Q4 Discuss the **ethical** issues involved in using **embryonic stem cells** to treat diseases.

....

....

....

Biology 1b — Evolution and Environment

Genetic Engineering

Q1   Billy has **cystic fibrosis**. Say briefly how genetic engineering could be used to help him.

....

....

Q2   Some people are **worried** about genetic engineering.

    a)   Explain why some people are concerned about genetic engineering.

....

....

    b)   Do you think that scientists should be carrying out genetic engineering? Explain your answer.

....

....

....

Q3   Fill in the gaps in the passage below to explain **how** genetic engineering is carried out.

The useful .... is 'cut' from the donor organism's chromosome using

.... The same .... are then used to cut the host

organism's chromosome and the useful .... is inserted. This technique is

known as gene ....

Q4   Explain how genetic engineering can be used to produce large amounts of human insulin in a short time.

....

....

Q5   Look carefully at this headline about a new type of **GM salmon**.

> **Monster food? Scientists insert a growth hormone gene and create fish that grow much faster than ever before!**

Some scientists have warned that the GM salmon should be tightly controlled so they don't escape into the sea. What might happen if the GM salmon were allowed to escape?

....

....

Genetic Engineering

Q6   Read the article below about **GM crops** and answer the questions that follow.

There are many reasons for genetically modifying crops. Two important reasons are to make them pest-resistant and to make them resistant to herbicides (weedkillers).

At the moment no one's growing any GM crops in the UK. Recently, though, some farmers took part in crop trials set up by the Government, to see what effects growing herbicide-tolerant GM crops might have on wildlife. There were four kinds of crops in the trials — beet, spring oilseed rape, maize and winter oilseed rape.

Fields of various sizes were chosen for the study. In each case, the farmer split one of their normal fields in half. They then grew a 'normal' crop in one half and its GM equivalent in the other. Apart from that, they did everything normally — ploughing the field, adding fertiliser etc. in the same way as they usually would. The only difference was with herbicides — with the GM crops, the

farmers followed instructions about how much of which herbicides to use, and when to apply them. They applied herbicides to the 'normal' crop as they usually would.

As the crops grew, the government researchers counted the number of weeds growing, and the number of weed seeds produced in each half of the field. They also monitored the populations of insects, slugs, spiders and other wildlife.

The researchers found that with three crops (beet, spring oilseed rape and winter oilseed rape), growing normal crops was better for wildlife — they found more butterflies and bees on the normal crops. They also found more flowering weeds (the kinds that butterflies and bees prefer) on the side with the normal crops. With maize, oddly, the opposite seemed to be true — there were more weeds, and more butterflies and bees, around the GM crops.

a)   Explain the **purpose** of the trial described in the article.

....

....

b)   i) Suggest why each field was divided in half rather than choosing separate fields for normal and GM crops.

....

....

Farmer Gideon had a brand new combine harvester and he wasn't going to give anyone the keys.

ii) Give two things that were done in the same way by the farmers for the GM crops and for the normal crops. Suggest why these things were kept constant.

....

....

iii) Give one thing that was done differently for the GM crops and for the normal crops. Suggest why this was not kept constant for both types of crop.

....

....

Genetic Engineering

c) Herbicides were used on **both** the normal and the GM crops in this trial.

    i) Explain why fewer weeds normally grow among herbicide-resistant crops.

       ....

       ....

    ii) Explain how growing herbicide-resistant crops in the UK could benefit:

       farmers. ....

       ....

       shoppers buying these products. ....

       ....

d) The result for the **maize** crop was surprising. Tick the box next to the **correct** statement below.

    ☐ The result was surprising because wildlife preferred the GM maize even though there were fewer weeds.

    ☐ The result was surprising because there were more weeds with the GM crop even though more herbicide was used.

    ☐ The result was surprising because bees and butterflies are usually repelled by GM crops.

e) Some people are **worried** that growing GM crops will lead to a reduction in **biodiversity**.

    i) Do you think that the results of this trial support the above fear? Explain your answer.

       ....

       ....

    ii) Give two other reasons why people are concerned about GM crops.

       ....

       ....

    iii) Suggest one possible reason for the unusual result seen with the maize crop in this trial.

       ....

       ....

Evolution

Q1 a) Roughly how many species have so far been identified on Earth?
Circle the correct number from the options listed below.

1500   15 000   150 000   1 500 000

b) There are actually many more species than this. Some scientists think there might be as many as 100 million species on Earth. Suggest why this figure is so much bigger than the figure in part a).

....

....

Q2 Dinosaurs, mammoths and dodos are all animals that are now **extinct.**

a) What does the term 'extinct' mean?

....

....

b) How do we know about extinct animals?

....

....

Q3 Fossils of shells were found in a sample of rock.

Think about what replaces the tissues of organisms as they slowly decay.

a) Explain how fossils form.

....

....

....

b) Why are fossils of animals more common than those of plants?

....

c) Fossils were found in this sample of rock.
Explain why scientists think that fossil B is older.

Fossil A

Fossil B

....

....

Top Tips: My biology teacher was a bit of an old fossil... expert. Some people think fossils are really boring (picture the reaction when Ross from Friends starts going on about them) but the fossil record has provided evidence of all kinds of weird and wonderful creatures that are now long gone. Think Tyrannosaurus rex and gigantic guinea pigs — wow.

Evolution

Q4 A and B are fossilised bones from the legs of ancestors of the modern horse. Some scientists believe that animals with legs like fossil A gradually developed into animals with legs like fossil B.

a) Suggest **two** reasons why this change may have happened.

....

....

....

....

b) It is thought that there was a stage in the development of the horse between A and B, during which the leg bone would have looked like C. Suggest why no fossils of C have been found.

....

....

Q5 One idea of **how life began** is that simple organic molecules were brought to Earth by **comets**. It's not known if this is right.

a) What do we call this type of scientific idea? ....

b) Suggest why this idea has neither been generally accepted or completely rejected by all scientists.

....

c) Give another scientific idea for how life began.

....

....

Q6 Some animals were exposed to a chemical which damaged the **DNA** in their **skin cells**. These animals developed skin cancer. They then had offspring, **none** of which developed skin cancer.

a) What do we call a change in DNA?

....

b) Why was the skin cancer not passed on to the offspring?

....

....

c) Some of the offspring had new mutations in the DNA in each of their cells. These had not been present in all the cells of their parents and were thought to be due to the chemical. Which cells in the bodies of the parent animals do you think had been damaged, other than the skin cells?

....

Evolution

Q7 Giraffes used to have much **shorter** necks than they do today.

a) The statements below explain Darwin's theory about how their neck length changed.
Write numbers in the boxes to show the **order** the statements should be in.

☐ The giraffes competed for food from low branches. This food started to become scarce. Many giraffes died before they could breed.

☐ More long-necked giraffes survived to breed, so more giraffes were born with long necks.

☐ A giraffe was born with a longer neck than normal. The long-necked giraffe was able to eat more food.

☐ All giraffes had short necks.

☐ The long-necked giraffe survived to have lots of offspring that all had longer necks.

☐ All giraffes had long necks.

b) Lamarck's theory of how giraffes evolved to have long necks was different from Darwin's. How would Lamarck have explained their evolution?

....

....

Q8 **Sickle cell anaemia** is a serious **genetic** disease that makes it harder for a person to carry enough oxygen in their blood. In Europe the disease is very **rare**. However, in Africa sickle cell anaemia is more **common**.

a) Explain why natural selection may act against people with sickle cell anaemia in Europe.

....

....

b) Malaria is also more common in Africa. People who carry a gene for sickle cell anaemia are more resistant to malaria. Explain how natural selection means there's more sickle cell anaemia in Africa.

....

....

Q9 A student incubated a sample of bacteria on an agar plate. The bacteria multiplied to form a plaque. He then added an **antibiotic** to the bacteria. Most of the bacteria died. He incubated the plate again and the remaining bacteria reproduced to form a new plaque. He added the **same** antibiotic to the bacterial plaque and **nothing happened**. Explain these results.

....

....

Human Impact on the Environment

Q1 Circle the correct word to complete each sentence below.

a) The size of the human population now is **bigger** / **smaller** than it was 1000 years ago.

b) The growth of the human population now is **slower** / **faster** than it was 1000 years ago.

c) The human impact on the environment now is **less** / **greater** than it was 1000 years ago.

Q2 The graph below shows the amount of sulfur dioxide released in the UK between 1970 and 2003.

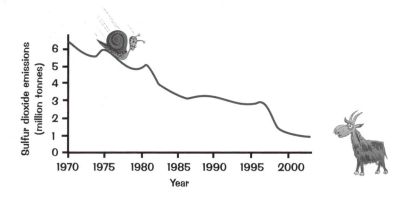

a) In which year shown on the graph were sulfur dioxide emissions highest? ....

b) Approximately how much sulfur dioxide was emitted in 2003? ....

c) Name one problem caused by sulfur dioxide.

    ....

Q3 One way to assess a person's impact on the Earth is to use an **ecological footprint**. This involves calculating **how many Earths** would be needed if everyone lived like that person. It takes into account things like the amount of **waste** the person produces and how much **energy** they use.

a) Two men calculate their ecological footprints. Eight Earths would be needed to support everyone in the way John lives. Half an Earth would be enough to support everyone in the way Derek lives.

  i) One of the men lives in a UK city, and one in rural Kenya. Who is more likely to live where?

      ....

  ii) Tick any of the following that are possible reasons for the difference in results.

    ☐ John buys more belongings, which use more raw materials to manufacture.

    ☐ John has central heating in his home but Derek has a wood fire.

    ☐ John throws away less waste.

    ☐ John drives a car and Derek rides a bicycle.

b) Suggest one thing John could do to reduce the size of his ecological footprint.

    ....

Human Impact on the Environment

Q4   The size of the Earth's population has an impact on our environment.

a)   Use the table below to plot a graph on the grid, showing how the world's human population has changed over the last 1000 years.

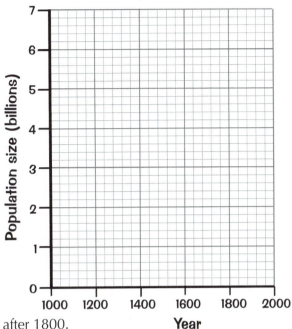

NO. OF PEOPLE (BILLIONS)	YEAR
0.3	1000
0.4	1200
0.4	1400
0.6	1600
1.0	1800
1.7	1900
6.1	2000

b)   Suggest two reasons for the sudden increase after 1800.

....

....

Q5   As the human population **grows** we need more **food**. Modern farming methods can increase the amount of food grown, but they may harm the environment.

a)   Give three types of chemicals used in modern farming.

1. ....

2. ....

3. ....

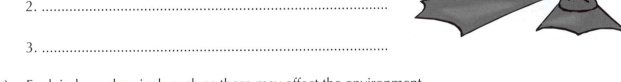

b)   Explain how chemicals such as these may affect the environment.

....

....

....

Top Tips:

There's lots to think about with this topic. It's the kind of thing you might get a longer answer question on in an exam, where you have to weigh up all the different arguments. And of course, examiners can't get enough of that graph where the human population suddenly goes shooting up — they love it.

The Greenhouse Effect

Q1 Underline the statements below about the greenhouse effect that are **true**.

The greenhouse effect is needed for life on Earth as we know it.

Greenhouse gases include carbon dioxide and sulfur dioxide.

The greenhouse effect causes acid rain.

Increasing amounts of greenhouse gases is causing global warming.

Q2 The Earth receives energy from the **Sun**. It radiates much of this energy back towards space.

a) Explain the role of the greenhouse gases in keeping the Earth warm.

....

....

b) What would happen if there were no greenhouse gases?

....

c) In recent years the amounts of greenhouse gases in the atmosphere have increased.
Explain how this leads to global warming.

....

....

Q3 **Deforestation** increases the amount of **carbon dioxide** released
into the atmosphere and decreases the amount removed.

a) Explain how this happens.

....

....

....

....

b) Give three reasons why humans cut forests down.

....

....

c) Give two other examples of human activities that release carbon dioxide into the atmosphere.

....

The Greenhouse Effect

Q4   The graph below shows changes in **global temperature** since 1859.

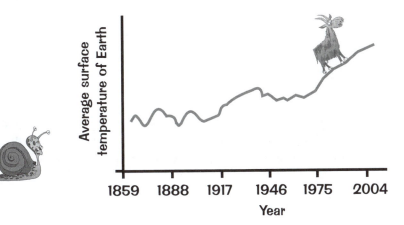

a)   Describe the trend shown on the graph.

....

b)   The next graph shows how current levels of three gases
compare to their levels before the Industrial Revolution.

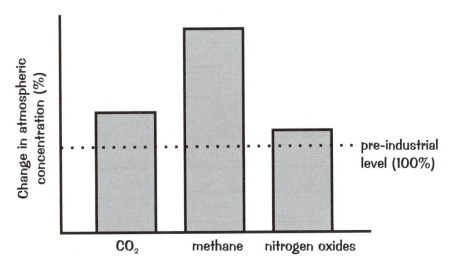

i)   Which gas has had the biggest percentage increase in concentration? ....

ii)   Give one source of this gas.

....

c)   What conclusion can you draw from these two graphs?
Did one of the changes definitely cause the other?

....

....

....

Climate Change

Q1 One UK newspaper said that global warming will be good for the UK because people will be able to have more barbecues. Do you think they're right? Explain your answer.

....

....

Q2 Two university students carried out **observations**. Student A noticed that a glacier was melting. Student B noticed that daffodils were flowering earlier in 2006 than in 2005. Both students concluded that this was due to **global warming**. Are they right? Explain your answer.

....

....

Q3 These statements help explain how **global warming** may lead to floods and temperature decreases. Use them to complete the **flow chart**, which has one box filled in to start you off.

Low-lying areas are at risk of flooding.   Some areas (maybe the UK) get colder.

Ocean currents are disrupted.   Higher temperatures make ice melt.

Cold fresh water enters the ocean.   Sea levels start to rise.

The seas get warmer and expand.

1

3

5

2

4

6

Q4 There's a **scientific consensus** that global warming is happening. This means scientists have collected enough **evidence** to support the **theory**.

a) What is meant by evidence and theory?

evidence: ....

theory: ....

b) Give examples of the sort of data that scientists are collecting about climate change.

....

....

Sustainable Development

Q1   Humans can affect the **environment** in lots of ways.

a)   Give two ways that humans can have a negative effect on the environment.

....

b)   Explain why some of the negative effects caused by humans cannot easily be reversed.

....

....

Q2   **Ecosystems** like rainforests contain many different **species**. If we destroy rainforests we risk making species extinct and **reducing biodiversity**.

a)   Define the term '**ecosystem**'. ....

....

b)   What is meant by '**reducing biodiversity**'?

....

c)   What are the implications for humans of reducing biodiversity?

....

....

....

Q3   Mayfly larvae and sludge worms are often studied to see how much **sewage** is in water.

a)   What is the name for an organism used in this way? ....

Juanita recorded the number of each species in water samples taken at three different distances away from a sewage outlet. Her results are shown on the right.

Distance (km)	No. of mayfly larvae	No. of sludge worms
1	3	20
2	11	14
3	23	7

b)   Give one thing that she would have to do to make this experiment a fair test.

....

c)   What can you conclude about the two organisms from these results?

....

....

d)   Suggest why sewage may decrease the number of mayfly larvae.

....

....

Mixed Questions — Biology 1b

Q1 The graph shows how the **body temperatures** of a camel and a goat change throughout the day in a hot desert.

a) Between 6 am and 12 noon, what happened to the body temperature:

   i) of the camel? ....

   ii) of the goat? ....

b) Which one of the animals keeps cool by sweating? ....

c) Explain why animals that use sweating to keep cool can't survive well in deserts.

   ....

d) Camels were a traditional means of transport in the desert. However, more people are now using 4-wheel-drive jeeps. Explain why a camel is a **more sustainable** form of transport than a jeep.

   ....

   ....

Q2 An experiment was done with two **fertilised natterjack toad eggs**. The eggs came from completely different parents. The nucleus of **egg A** was put into **egg B**, and the nucleus of egg B was **removed** (see the diagram on the right).

Nucleus from A is inserted into B   Nucleus from B is discarded

a) Egg **B** grew into a toad. Would you expect it to look more like the parents of egg **A** or the parents of egg **B**? Explain your answer.

   ....

b) The technique used to create Dolly the sheep also involved removing genetic material from an egg cell. However, Dolly was a **clone**, whereas the toad produced in this experiment was not. Explain why this is.

   ....

   ....

c) There are now far fewer natterjack toads than there were a century ago. This is largely due to **human impact**. Suggest **two** ways that humans may have caused their numbers to decline.

   ....

   ....

d) **Competition** with other amphibians has also had an effect on the number of natterjack toads. Suggest **two** things that the toads may have been competing for.

   ....

e) Because of their permeable skin, amphibians are '**sensitive indicator species**'. Explain what this term means. ....

   ....

Mixed Questions — Biology 1b

Q3 The table shows four people, identified by the letters **M**, **Q**, **X** and **Z**.

Characteristic	Code-name			
	M	Q	X	Z
They have a suntan	✓	✓		
They are male	✓	✓	✓	
They can roll their tongue	✓		✓	
Natural hair colour is brown	✓	✓	✓	✓
They have bleached blond hair			✓	✓
They have brown eyes	✓	✓	✓	

a) Use the information in the table to identify which two people could be identical twins.

....

b) Explain your answer.

....

....

Q4 The normal numbers of **chromosomes** in the body cells of some different species are:

> donkeys — 31 pairs of chromosomes   horses — 32 pairs of chromosomes
>
> lions — 19 pairs of chromosomes   tigers — 19 pairs of chromosomes

Mating between different, closely-related species occasionally results in offspring. However, the offspring are usually **sterile**. For example, a **mule** is a cross between a donkey and a horse, and a **liger** is a cross between a lion and a tiger.

a) Use the information above to work out the number of chromosomes in the body cells of a mule.

Hint: Think about the number of chromosomes in the gametes of donkeys and horses.

....

b) Mules are almost always sterile, but ligers can occasionally produce offspring of their own. Explain this by considering the number of chromosomes of ligers and mules.

....

....

Q5 Scientists tried to **genetically modify** some bacteria. They inserted a piece of DNA containing both the human gene for **growth hormone** and a gene for **penicillin resistance** into a bacterium. Afterwards, the bacteria were grown on agar plates containing penicillin.

a) Why were the bacteria grown on plates containing penicillin?

Hint: It's hard to tell by looking if the growth hormone gene has been inserted correctly.

....

....

b) Give **two advantages** of producing growth hormone with bacteria, rather than by other methods.

....

....

c) The bacteria produced were all genetically identical. What type of reproduction do you think took place?

....

Mixed Questions — Biology 1b

Q6   In the Galapagos Islands, different varieties of **giant tortoise** are found on different islands. For example, where the main available food is grass, the tortoises have a dome-shaped shell. However, where the main food is tall cacti, the tortoises have a saddle-backed shell, which allows them to raise their heads higher to feed.

dome-shelled tortoise   saddle-back tortoise

a)   Charles Darwin was particularly interested in animals like the tortoise on the Galapagos Islands. Explain the significance of these animals for Darwin.

....

....

b)   Why do islands often have their own species of animals?

....

....

c)   Explain the difference between **evolution** and **natural selection**.

....

....

d)   The Galapagos Islands have been described as an '**oasis for biodiversity**'. Explain what this means.

....

e)   **Galapagos penguins** are the rarest **penguins** in the world. Their numbers have fallen in recent years and scientists believe that this is partly due to **changing ocean currents**, which have affected the penguins' food sources. Explain how **humans** are contributing to this problem.

....

....

f)   The Galapagos Islands are becoming an increasingly popular tourist destination, but visitors to the islands can damage the fragile ecosystems. There are calls for tourism in the Galapagos Islands to be '**sustainably developed**'. Explain what is meant by this phrase.

....

....

g)   There is a rule which forbids tourists from bringing '**any live material**' to the Galapagos Islands. Suggest why this is.

....

....

Life and Cells

Q1 Sort the following list by writing each term in the correct place in the table below.

sperm   blood   digestive system   tree
cat   liver   egg (human)   stomach
reproductive system   muscle   eye   fungus
excretory system   white blood cell   heart   leaf

Cell	Tissue	Organ	Organ system	Organism

Q2 State what the following cell structures **contain** or are **made of** and what their **functions** are.

a) The **nucleus** contains ....

Its function is ....

b) **Chloroplasts** contain ....

Their function is ....

c) The **cell wall** is made of ....

Its function is ....

Q3 Tick the boxes to show whether the following statements are **true** or **false**.

		True	False
a)	A leaf is an organ.	☐	☐
b)	Organisms have only one organ system.	☐	☐
c)	Palisade cells are present in leaf tissue.	☐	☐
d)	Mitochondria are where most of the respiration reactions take place.	☐	☐
e)	A heart contains different types of tissue.	☐	☐

Q4 Plant and animal cells have **similarities** and **differences**.
Complete each statement below by choosing the correct words.

a) **Plant** / **animal** cells, but not **plant** / **animal** cells, contain chloroplasts.

b) Plant cells have a **vacuole** / **cell wall**, which is made of cellulose.

c) **Both plant and animal cells** / **Only plant cells** / **Only animal cells** contain mitochondria.

d) Chloroplasts are where **respiration** / **photosynthesis** occurs, which makes **glucose** / **water**.

Specialised Cells

Q1 Give the correct name for each of the specialised cells described below.

a) These cells transport oxygen around the body. ....

b) Cells with many chloroplasts for photosynthesis. ....

c) The male reproductive cell. ....

d) Cells that open and close stomata on leaves. ....

e) The female reproductive cell. ....

Q2 Below are three features of **palisade leaf cells**. Draw lines to match each feature to its function.

Lots of chloroplasts	gives a large surface area for absorbing CO_2
Tall shape	means you can pack more cells in at the top of the leaf
Thin shape	for photosynthesis

Q3 Complete the following paragraph about **guard cells**, using the words below.

night   turgid   flaccid   photosynthesis   stomata

Guard cells open and close the .... When the plant has lots of water the

guard cells are .... This makes the stomata open, so gases can be exchanged for

.... When the plant is short of water the guard cells become

..........................., making the stomata close. They also close at .... to save water.

Q4 Red blood cells are adapted to **carry oxygen**.

a) What **shape** are red blood cells? ....

b) How does the shape of the cell help it carry oxygen?

....

c) Why do the cells have **no nucleus**?

....

Q5 Below is a list of features of **reproductive cells**. Decide which ones are found in **sperm** cells and which ones are found in **egg** cells.

	Sperm	Egg
a) A long tail	☐	☐
b) Enzymes to digest cell membranes	☐	☐
c) A large food reserve	☐	☐
d) Lots of mitochondria	☐	☐
e) A streamlined head	☐	☐

Diffusion

Q1   Complete the passage below by choosing the most appropriate words.

> Diffusion is the **direct** / **random** movement of particles from an area where they are at a
> **higher** / **lower** concentration to an area where they are at a **higher** / **lower** concentration.
> The rate of diffusion is faster when the concentration gradient is **bigger** / **smaller** and in
> **liquids** / **gases**. It is slower when there is a **large** / **small** distance over which
> diffusion occurs and when there is **more** / **less** surface for diffusion to take place.

Q2   The first diagram below shows a **cup of tea** which has just had a **sugar cube** added.

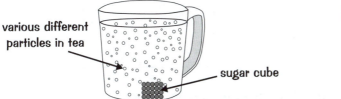

various different particles in tea

sugar cube

a)   In the second cup above, draw the appearance of the molecules of **sugar** in the tea after an hour.

b)   Predict how the rate of diffusion of the sugar would change in each of the following situations:

i) sugar crystals are used rather than a sugar cube

....

ii) the tea is heated

....

iii) the sugar and tea are placed in a long thin tube

....

c)   Explain the movement of the sugar particles in terms of areas of different concentration.

....

....

Q3   Patsy was studying in her bedroom. Her dad was cooking curry for tea in
the kitchen. Soon Patsy could smell the curry that her dad was making.

a)   Her dad was warm so he switched on a fan. Suggest what effect the
fan would have on the rate that the curry particles spread through the house.

....

b)   After tasting the curry, Patsy's dad added more curry powder. What effect would this
have on the smell of the curry? Explain your answer using the word **concentration**.

....

....

Diffusion

Q4 Some statements about **diffusion** are written below.
Decide which are correct and then write **true** or **false** in the spaces.

a) Diffusion takes place in all types of substances. ....

b) Diffusion is usually quicker in liquids than in gases. ....

c) Diffusion happens more quickly when there is a higher concentration gradient. ....

d) A larger surface area makes diffusion happen more quickly. ....

e) When there is a larger distance this speeds up the rate of diffusion. ....

Q5 Two models of diffusion are shown below.

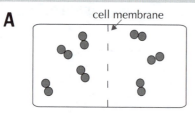
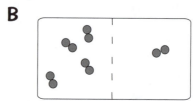

a) Would you expect the molecules to diffuse **faster** in situation A or B? ....

b) Explain your answer.

....

Q6 Phil was investigating the diffusion of **glucose** and **starch** through a **membrane**.
He placed equal amounts of glucose solution and starch solution inside a bag
designed to act like a cell membrane. He then put the bag into a beaker of water.

a) After 20 minutes, Phil tested the water for the presence
of starch and glucose. Circle which of the following you
would expect to be found in the water outside the bag:

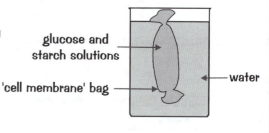

glucose   **starch**

b) Explain your answer to part a).

....

....

c) Phil did the experiment again using the same amounts of glucose
and starch solutions. This time he used a much longer, thinner bag.

Will the diffusion happen faster or more slowly this time?
Explain your answer.

....

....

Think about the surface areas of the bags.

Top Tips: Don't forget it's only small molecules that can diffuse through cell membranes, e.g.
glucose, amino acids, water and oxygen. Big hulking things like proteins and starch can't fit through.

Biology 2(i) — Life Processes

Osmosis

Q1   This diagram shows a tank separated into two by a partially permeable membrane.

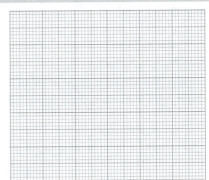

| Water molecule |
| Sugar molecule |

a) On which side of the membrane is there the higher concentration of water molecules?

....

b) In which direction would you expect more water molecules to travel — from A to B or from B to A?

....

c) Predict whether the level of liquid on side B will **rise** or **fall**. Explain your answer.

The liquid level on side B will ...., because ....

....

Q2   Some **potato cylinders** were placed in solutions of different **salt concentrations**. At the start of the experiment each cylinder was 50 mm long. Their final lengths are recorded in the table below.

Concentration of salt (molar)	Final length of potato cylinder (mm)	Change in length of potato cylinder (mm)
0	60	
0.25	58	
0.5	56	
0.75	70	
1	50	
1.25	45	

a) Plot the points for concentration of salt solution vs final length of potato cylinders on the grid.

b) Work out the change in length of each of the cylinders and complete the table above.

c) Study the pattern of the results.

    i) State the salt concentration(s) that produced unexpected results. ....

    ii) Suggest a method for deciding which of the results are correct.

....

d) State **three** factors that should have been kept constant to ensure this was a fair test.

....

....

....

Biology 2(i) — Life Processes

58

Osmosis

Q3 The diagram below shows some **body cells** bathed in **tissue fluid**. A blood vessel flows close to the cells, providing water. The cells shown have a low concentration of water inside them.

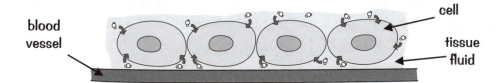

a) Is the concentration of water higher in the **tissue fluid** or inside the **cells**?

....

b) In which direction would you expect more water to travel — **into** the cells or **out of** the cells? Explain your answer.

....

....

c) Explain why osmosis appears to stop after a while.

....

Q4 Joan was making a meal of **salted ham** and **fruit salad**. She covered the meat in water and left it to soak for a few hours. When she returned, the meat was much bigger in size.

a) Use the term **osmosis** to help you explain the change in appearance of the ham.

....

....

b) To make her fruit salad, Joan cut some oranges, raisins and sultanas, sprinkled sugar over them and left them overnight. When she examined the fruit next morning they were surrounded by a **liquid**.

i) Suggest what the liquid might be. ....

ii) Explain where the liquid has come from.

....

iii) Joan then washed the fruit and observed that the raisins and sultanas once again became swollen. Explain what has happened this time.

....

....

Biology 2(i) — Life Processes

Photosynthesis

Q1   **Photosynthesis** is the process that produces 'food' in plants.
Use some of the words below to complete the equation for photosynthesis.

oxygen   carbon dioxide   nitrogen   water   glucose   sodium chloride

$$\text{.......................} + \text{.......................} \xrightarrow[\text{chlorophyll}]{\text{sunlight}} \text{.......................} + \text{.......................}$$

Q2   The rate of photosynthesis in some pondweed was recorded by counting
the bubbles produced per minute at equal intervals during the day.

No. bubbles per minute	Time of day
0	06.00
10	12.00
20	18.00
0	

a)   The time for the final reading is missing.
Predict what the time is likely to be.

....

b)   Explain why the rate of photosynthesis is 0 bubbles per minute for this time of day.

....

c)   Suggest where plants get their food from at this time of day.

....

d)   Plot a bar graph on the grid on the right to
display the results shown on the table.

Don't forget about the scales on your graph.

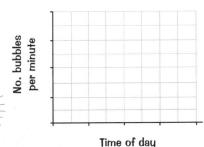

Q3   The graph below shows the **oxygen** and **carbon dioxide** exchanged by a plant.
The concentration of each gas was measured next to the leaves as light intensity increased.

a)   **i)**   Which gas is oxygen and which is carbon dioxide?

Gas A is   ....

Gas B is   ....

ii) Explain how you decided.

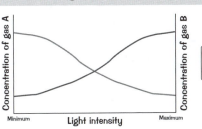

....

....

b)   State the relationships between the following:

i)   the light intensity and the concentration of carbon dioxide.

....

ii) the light intensity and the concentration of oxygen.

....

Photosynthesis

Q4   Jack conducted an experiment to investigate the effect of light on photosynthesis. He placed one plant (plant A) in the **dark** for 24 hours, and another plant (plant B) in bright **sunlight**. Jack tested a leaf from each plant for **starch**.

Plant A   Plant B

a)   Which plant would you expect to contain more starch?

....

b)   Explain your answer to part a) above.

....

....

c)   Where in the palisade cells of leaves does photosynthesis happen? ....

Q5   A diagram of a leaf in cross-section is shown below.

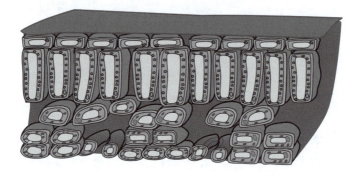

Suggest how each of the following features of the leaf are important for photosynthesis:

a)   The leaf has a **flat surface**.

....

b)   The leaf is **thin**.

....

c)   The leaf is **green**.

....

d)   There are **pores** on the surface of the leaf.

....

The Rate of Photosynthesis

Q1   Below are some straightforward questions about **limiting factors**. Hooray.

   a)   List **three** factors that can limit the rate of photosynthesis.

   ....

   b)   Explain the meaning of the term "limiting factor".

   ....

   c)   The limiting factor at a particular time depends on the environmental conditions, e.g. season (such as winter). Name two other environmental conditions that may affect the rate of photosynthesis.

   ....

Q2   Choose the most appropriate word to complete the following statements.

   a)   The rate of photosynthesis depends on the availability of **raw materials / products**.

   b)   When photosynthesis is taking place **quickly / slowly**, more oxygen gas is being produced.

   c)   The rate of photosynthesis cannot be speeded up beyond **an optimal / a minor** rate.

Q3   Seth investigated the effect of different concentrations of **carbon dioxide** on the rate of photosynthesis of his Swiss cheese plant. The results are shown on the graph below.

   a)   What effect does increasing the concentration of CO_2 have on the rate of photosynthesis?

   ....

   ....

   ....

   ....

   b)   Explain why all the graphs level off eventually.

   ....

Think about the third limiting factor.

   ....

Q4   Sunlight contains light of different **wavelengths**, some of which we see as different **colours**. The amount of light absorbed at each wavelength for the green pigment **chlorophyll** is shown below.

   a)   What wavelengths and colours of light are best absorbed by chlorophyll?

   ....

   ....

   b)   Suggest how you could use the information on the graph to increase the growth rate of plants in a greenhouse.

   ....

The Rate of Photosynthesis

Q5   Lucy investigated the **volume of oxygen** produced by pondweed at **different intensities of light**. Her results are shown in the table below.

Relative light intensity	1	2	3	4	5
Volume of oxygen evolved in 10 minutes (ml)	12	25	13	48	61

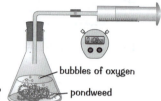

bubbles of oxygen

pondweed

a)   What was Lucy measuring by recording the volume of oxygen produced?

....

b)   Plot a graph of her results.

c) **i)** One of Lucy's results is probably wrong. Circle this point on the graph.

  ii) Suggest what error Lucy might have made when she collected this result.

....

....

....

d)   Describe the relationship shown on the graph between light intensity and photosynthesis rate.

....

....

e)   Would you expect this relationship to continue if Lucy continued to increase the light intensity? Explain your answer.

....

....

Q6   Farmer Fred doesn't put his cows out during the winter because the grass is not growing.

a)   State **two** differences between summer and winter conditions that affect the rate of photosynthesis in the grass.

1. ....

2. ....

b)   How are the rate of photosynthesis and the growth rate of grass related?

....

....

Biology 2(i) — Life Processes

The Rate of Photosynthesis

Q7   Graham decided to build a **greenhouse** to grow his plants in.

a)   List **three** reasons why a greenhouse is an ideal environment for growing plants.

....

....

....

b)   i)   What could Graham add to his greenhouse in the **winter** for better growth?

....

ii)   What should he add in the **summer** to ensure it doesn't get too hot?

....

iii)   What addition would be useful at **night** if he wants the plants to continue photosynthesising?

....

iv)   Why might it be better to install a **paraffin heater** rather than an electric heater?

....

Q8   Average daytime summer temperatures in different habitats around the world are recorded in the table below.

Habitat	Temperature (°C)
Forest	19
Arctic	0
Desert	32
Grassland	22
Rainforest	27

a)   Plot a **bar chart** for these results on the grid.

b)   From the values for temperature, in which area would you expect fewest plants to grow?

....

c)   Suggest a reason for your answer above using the terms **enzymes** and **photosynthesis**.

....

....

d)   **Explain** why very few plants can usually grow in the desert even though it has a much higher average temperature than the rainforest where many varieties of plants can grow.

....

....

How Plants Use the Glucose

Q1 Complete the passage below by choosing the most appropriate words from the list below.

convert	fruits	leaves	fructose	cells	cellulose
energy	walls	sucrose	lipids	margarine	

Plants make glucose in their .... Some of it is used for respiration,

which releases .... and allows the plant to ....

the rest of the glucose into other substances and build new ....

Some plants store glucose in .... which get eaten by animals.

To do this, glucose and another sugar called .... are turned into

.... In rapidly growing plants, glucose is also converted into

.... to build cell .... Seeds can store glucose in

the form of ...., which we use to make ....

Q2 Plants use glucose to make **protein**. Humans eat plants and animals as sources of protein. Below is a graph comparing the nutrients in dhal and steak, including their protein content.

a) What percentage of your recommended daily allowance of protein is provided by 100 g of the following?

dhal ....

steak ....

Dhal is just lentils.

Comparison of nutrients in dhal and steak

b) Which of these two foods provides a better source of dietary nutrients in general? Explain your choice.

....

....

c) Suggest where the protein found in steak originally came from.

....

Q3 New potato plants are grown from potato **tubers**, which are stores of **starch**.

a) Suggest how the new plants obtain the energy needed for growth.

....

b) Explain why the plants no longer need this energy source once they have grown above the soil.

....

c) Why do the tubers store starch, not glucose?

....

Minerals for Healthy Growth

Q1 Draw lines to match each of the following **minerals** with their **functions** in plants.

MAGNESIUM

NITRATES

for making proteins

for making chlorophyll

Q2 An investigation into the **mineral requirements** of plants was carried out as shown below.

tubes 1 and 2:   complete mineral content
tubes 3 and 4:   lacking nitrates
tubes 5 and 6:   lacking magnesium

a) Suggest why tubes 1 and 2 were included.

....

b) Predict how the seedlings in the following tubes will grow:

i) 3 and 4   ....

ii) 5 and 6   ....

c) Suggest why all the minerals required **except one** were supplied to tubes 3, 4, 5 and 6.

....

....

Q3 The levels of **magnesium** in fruit and vegetables tested in 1930 and 1980 are shown below.

Plant	Magnesium content (%)		Change (%)
	1930	1980	
Brussel sprouts	19	8	
Carrots	12	3	
Onions	7.4	4	
Peas	30.2	34	
Potatoes	24.2	17	
Tomatoes	11	7	
Bananas	41.9	34	
Apples	4.7	3	
Strawberries	11.7	10	

a) Calculate the % change in magnesium content for each type of plant. Write your answers in the table.

Change in level = Final level minus initial level

b) State the general trend shown in the magnesium content.

....

c) How could you identify plants **deficient** in magnesium?

....

....

d) What term describes repeatedly growing a single type of plant in the same field? ....

e) Suggest what may have caused the trend shown in the table.

Think about how your answer to part d) affects the soil.

....

....

Pyramids of Number and Biomass

Q1 Place **ticks** in the right columns to say which features apply to pyramids of **numbers** or **biomass**. For each feature, you might need to tick one column, both, or none at all.

Feature	Pyramid of numbers	Pyramid of biomass
Values for mass are shown at each level.		
Nearly always a pyramid shape.		
Each bar represents a step in a food chain.		
Always starts with a producer.		
Can only have 3 steps.		
Numbers are shown at each step.		

Q2 A single **robin** has a mass of 15 g and eats caterpillars. Each robin eats 25 **caterpillars** that each have a mass of 2 g. The caterpillars feed on 10 **stinging nettles** that together have a mass of 500 g. Study the pyramid diagrams shown then answer the questions that follow.

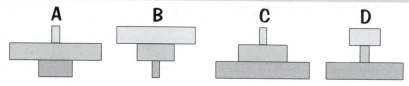

A **B** **C** **D**

a) Which diagram is most likely to represent a pyramid of **numbers** for these organisms? ....

b) Which is most likely to represent a pyramid of **biomass** for these organisms? ....

c) Explain how you decided on your answer to part b) above.

....

d) The stinging nettles are the first trophic level. Where does their energy initially come from?

....

Q3 In the 1950s a chemical called **DDT** was used to control animal pests. DDT was later discovered to be toxic and was detected at very high levels in organisms across food chains, as shown below.

a) Describe what happens to the level of DDT found in organisms as you go up the trophic levels.

....

....

Osprey (13.8 ppm DDT)
Pike (2.8 ppm DDT)
Silverside fish (0.23 ppm DDT)
Algae (0.04 ppm DDT)

'ppm' = 'parts per million'

b) Work out by how many times (e.g. 2 times or 70 times) the level of DDT has risen in the following:

  i) in the top consumer compared with the producer ....

  ii) in the secondary consumer compared with the producer ....

c) Suggest why a pyramid of biomass is a suitable diagram for displaying the problem with DDT.

....

Energy Transfer and Decay

Q1 Indicate whether these statements are **true** or **false**.

True False

a) Without sunlight, nearly all life on Earth would die. ☐ ☐

b) Food chains generally have no more than five steps. ☐ ☐

c) Materials are not lost from food chains — they are recycled. ☐ ☐

d) Elements like carbon are passed across food chains. ☐ ☐

e) Energy only is passed between the steps of food chains. ☐ ☐

f) Food chains that include animals with constant body temperatures are less likely to lose energy as heat. ☐ ☐

Q2 Look at the picture of the **compost bin** below. Then choose **three** of the features shown and explain how each feature aids the process of decomposition.

decomposers
open top
shredded waste
mesh sides
base in contact with soil

Feature	How it aids decomposition

Q3 Complete the sentences below by circling the correct words.

a) Nearly all life on Earth depends on **food / energy** from the Sun.

b) **Plants / Animals** can make their own food by a process called **photosynthesis / respiration**.

c) To obtain energy animals must **decay / eat** plant material or other animals.

d) Animals and plants release energy through the process of **photosynthesis / respiration**.

e) Some of the energy produced in animals is **gained / lost** through **growth / movement** before it reaches organisms at later steps of the food chain.

f) Some energy is lost between steps of a food chain because it's used to make **edible / inedible** materials such as **hair / flesh**.

Q4 The sentences below describe how **elements** are **recycled** in a food chain. Sort them into the correct order by numbering them 1 to 6. The first one has been done for you.

☐ Energy released in respiration is lost by decay, heat and movement and the production of waste.

☐ Materials are recycled and returned to the soil by decay.

☐1 Plants take up minerals from the soil.

☐ Plants use minerals and the products of photosynthesis to make complex nutrients.

☐ Nutrients in plants are passed to animals through feeding and used in respiration to provide energy.

☐ Waste and dead tissues are decayed by microorganisms.

Energy Transfer and Decay

Q5 Living things are made from materials that they take from the world around them.

  a) **i)** Name four **elements** that living organisms contain.

....

       ii) Where do organisms get these elements?

....

  b) Explain how the elements inside organisms are returned to the environment.

....

....

Q6 In a **stable community**, the materials that are taken out of the soil and used are balanced by those that are put back in. Decide whether each of the following examples describes a stable community or not — write **stable** or **not stable** in the spaces provided.

  a) A farmer plants a field of wheat. In Autumn he harvests the crop. ....

  b) In Autumn leaves fall from trees to the grass below where they decay. ....

  c) James rakes up the leaves on the ground of his orchard. ....

  d) When Julie mows the lawn she leaves the cuttings on the lawn's surface. ....

  e) Graham spreads manure from his neighbour's cows on his rose bed. ....

Q7 Study the diagram of **energy transfer** shown below.

Sun 103 500 kJ

Grass 2070 kJ

Rabbits 100 kJ   **A**   **Cows** 90 kJ

B 60 kJ   **C** 21 kJ

Humans

  a) Using the figures shown on the diagram, work out the percentage of the Sun's energy that is passed to the producer.

....

  b) The organisms at **A** are responsible for returning waste materials to the environment.

       i) What are these organisms? ....

       ii) Only 10% of the energy in the grass reaches the next trophic level. Work out how much of the producers' energy passes to them.

....

  c) **B** and **C** are processes that represent energy loss. Suggest what these processes might be.

....

  d) Why do food chains rarely have more than five trophic levels?

....

....

Managing Food Production

Q1 Three different **food chains** are shown here.

Grass → Cattle → Human

Pondweed → Small fish → Salmon → Human

Wheat → Human

a) Circle the food chain that shows the most **efficient** production of **food** for **humans**.

b) Explain your choice.

....

....

Q2 Complete the following passage by choosing words from the list below to fill in the gaps.

crowded   intensively   antibiotics   cheaper   efficiency   disease

In order to improve the .... of food production and so make

.... food for us, animals are often .... farmed.

This means they live in .... conditions where ....

spreads easily. To prevent this, animals are often given ....

Q3 The structure of the UK **egg industry** has changed in recent years. The table below shows the percentages of the egg market represented by three methods of chicken farming — **laying** (battery hens), **barn** (hens that roam freely indoors) and **free range** (hens that roam freely outdoors).

Year	Percentage of egg market for each type of chicken farming		
	Laying	Barn	Free range
1999	78	6	16
2001	72	5	23
2003	69	6	25
2005	66	7	27
Change			

a) Use the figures above to make a bar chart on the grid opposite.

b) Explain why battery farming has always been the most common method of chicken farming.

....

....

c) Calculate the change in the percentage of the market held by each farming type between 1999 and 2005. Write your answers in the spaces on the table. *final % - initial %*

d) Suggest a reason for the changes.

....

....

Organic Farming

Q1   Read the following passage about organic farming.

Why does organic food cost so much? Well, it costs more for the farmer to grow things, partly because it's more labour-intensive. Organic farmers don't use herbicides — so they have to pay people to weed their carrots, say, by hand. The use of pesticides is also restricted in organic farming — so the organic farmer risks losing his crops when they get munched up by pests like slugs.

The yield from organic agriculture is lower than from conventional farming. In other words, you get fewer carrots per acre of field. Organic methods rely on growing healthy plants and animals at an unforced pace. For instance, intensively farmed pigs are fed antibiotics which prevent the spread of disease, but which also make them grow faster. Organically farmed pigs are just fed pig food — so they take longer to grow fat and become ready for slaughter. Also, organically produced animals are given space to roam around. Intensively farmed animals are confined in small cages — this uses much less land, so it's cheaper.

So why pay all that extra money — is intensive farming so dreadful? Well, if you like to hear birds singing, and see wild flowers and butterflies, blasting the countryside with weedkiller and pesticides is probably not wise. And 'factory farming' isn't much fun if you're a pig or a chicken. It's cheap of course, but it could bring trouble in the long run. Will cheap sausages seem such a clever idea when people start dying because antibiotics don't work any more?

a) What two products are organic farmers not allowed to use?

....

b) Give **three** reasons why organic food is more expensive than its non-organic equivalent.

1. ....

2. ....

3. ....

c) Describe **one** difference between the life of an organically reared pig and an intensively farmed pig.

....

d) Many governments are currently trying to encourage farmers to adopt organic farming practices.

i) Give **one** reason why a government might be trying to increase the number of organic farms.

....

ii) State **two** reasons why many farmers don't change from intensive to organic farming.

1. ....

2. ....

e) Explain how certain intensive farming practices could lead to antibiotic resistance in bacteria that infect humans.

....

....

....

The Carbon Cycle

Q1 Complete the passage by inserting the most appropriate words from the list below.

respiration   carbohydrates   microorganisms   carbon dioxide

detritus   photosynthesis   eating   waste

Green plants remove .... from the air and use it in ....

At night plants return this gas to the air through ...., a process that occurs at

all times in living organisms including animals and .... Animals obtain a

supply of carbon by .... plants. Through digestion, carbon is released from

fats, proteins and .... that are stored in plant tissues. Carbon is released

from dead tissues and animal .... by .... feeders.

Q2 Draw lines to match the statements below with their correct endings.

Plants use...   carbon by photosynthesis.

Microorganisms release...   carbon dioxide by decaying waste and dead tissue.

Animals and plants release...   carbon through feeding.

Animals take in...   carbon dioxide to build complex molecules.

Plants take in...   carbon dioxide through respiration.

Q3 The pie chart below shows where stores of **carbon** are found on Earth.

150 745 680
.1390
960

□ ocean sediment
■ atmosphere
□ vegetation
■ soil
■ surface ocean
□ deep ocean

38100

Carbon stores on Earth (in gigatons)

a) State where the largest stores of carbon are held.

....

b) Calculate the total amount of carbon present in soil and vegetation. Show your working.

....

c) What **percentage** of the total carbon is contained in all parts of the ocean? Show your working.

....

d) State **two** processes that increase the levels of carbon dioxide in the atmosphere.

1. ....   2. ....

e) Increased carbon dioxide in the atmosphere is a major cause of climate change.
Explain one way that we could reduce the risk of climate change.

....

....

Mixed Questions — Biology 2(i)

Q1 The following cells are specialised to do their jobs. State **one** visible **feature** of each cell shown and explain **how it helps** the cell to do its job.

a) **Red blood cell**

i) Feature: ....

ii) Function of this feature: ....

....

b) **Palisade cell**

i) Feature: ....

ii) Function of this feature: ....

....

Q2 A student was given **three solutions** labelled X, Y and Z. He set up the experiment shown below and left it for a day. At the end of the experiment, the water outside the membrane contained particles X and Y, but not Z.

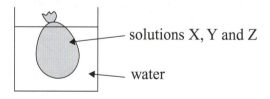

solutions X, Y and Z

water

a) Name the process by which particles of X and Y moved through the membrane.

....

b) What can you conclude about the relative sizes of the X, Y and Z particles?

....

c) Solutions X, Y and Z were in fact amino acid, protein and glucose solutions. Which of these solutions was substance Z?

....

Mixed Questions — Biology 2(i)

Q3 Diagrams A, B, C, D and E show some different **pyramids of number** and **pyramids of biomass**.

A   B

C   D   E

a) Which of the pyramids above **could not** be pyramids of biomass? Explain why.

....

....

....

....

b) Which of the pyramids could represent the following food chains?

i) Oak tree ➔ caterpillars ➔ blackbirds ➔ buzzards

....

ii) Potatoes ➔ humans

....

c) Why is it unusual to find food chains with more than five trophic levels?

....

....

....

Q4 a) Plants use photosynthesis to produce glucose. Give **two uses** of glucose for plants.

1. ....

2. ....

b) Why do plants convert glucose into **starch** for storage?

....

....

Biological Catalysts — Enzymes

Q1 a) Write a definition of the word '**enzyme**'.

....

b) In the space below, draw a sketch to show how an enzyme's **shape** allows it to break substances down.

Q2 This graph shows the results from an investigation into the effect of **temperature** on the rate of an **enzyme** catalysed reaction.

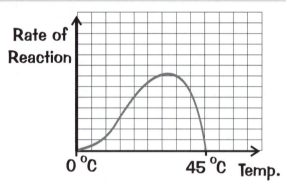

a) What is the **optimum** temperature for this enzyme?

....

b) What happens to enzymes at temperatures **above** their optimum?

....

Q3 a) Tick the correct boxes to show whether the sentences are true or false.

True **False**

i) Most enzymes are made of fat. ☐ ☐

ii) The rate of most chemical reactions can be increased by increasing the temperature. ☐ ☐

iii) Most cells are damaged at very high temperatures. ☐ ☐

iv) Each type of enzyme can speed up a lot of different reactions. ☐ ☐

b) Write a correct version of each false sentence in the space below.

....

....

Biological Catalysts — Enzymes

Q4   Stuart has a sample of an enzyme and he is trying to find out what its **optimum pH** is. Stuart tests the enzyme by **timing** how long it takes to break down a substance at different pH levels. The results of Stuart's experiment are shown below.

pH	time taken for reaction in seconds
2	101
4	83
6	17
8	76
10	99
12	102

a)   Draw a line graph of the results on the grid below.

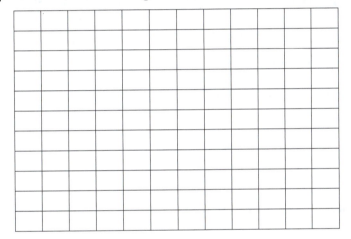

b)   Roughly what is the **optimum** pH for the enzyme?

   ....

c)   Explain why the reaction is very slow at certain pH levels.

   ....

d)   Would you expect to find this enzyme in the stomach? Explain your answer.

   ....

e)   Describe two things that Stuart would need to do to make sure his experiment is a fair test.

   1. ....

   2. ....

Top Tips: Enzymes crop up a lot in Biology so it's worth spending plenty of time making sure you know all the basics. If you're finding things a bit dull, you could always take a little break and eat some tofu to make sure you have enough protein to make lots of delightful enzymes.

Enzymes and Respiration

Q1 a)   Circle the correct word equation for **aerobic respiration**.

glucose + oxygen → carbon dioxide + water (+ energy)

protein + oxygen → carbon dioxide + water (+ energy)

glucose + carbon dioxide → oxygen + water (+ energy)

b)   What does the term 'aerobic respiration' mean?

....

Q2 a)   Tick the correct boxes to show whether the sentences are true or false.

True   False

i)   Aerobic respiration releases energy.   ☐ ☐

ii)   Respiration usually releases energy from protein.   ☐ ☐

iii)   Aerobic respiration is more efficient than anaerobic respiration.   ☐ ☐

iv)   Respiration takes place in a cell's nucleus.   ☐ ☐

v)   Aerobic respiration produces carbon dioxide.   ☐ ☐

vi)   Breathing is a kind of respiration.   ☐ ☐

vii)   Plants use photosynthesis instead of respiration.   ☐ ☐

b)   Write a correct version of each false sentence in the space below.

....

....

....

....

Q3   Give **four** examples of things that animals and / or plants use **energy** for.

1. ....

2. ....

3. ....

4. ....

Top Tips: Hmm, respiration, there isn't really much to say other than make sure you learn the word equation and remember that IT'S NOT THE SAME AS BREATHING.

Enzymes and Digestion

Q1   Fill in the boxes to show how the **three main food groups** are **broken down** during digestion.

a)

☐

protein ⟶ ☐

b)

lipase

☐ ⟶ ☐ + ☐

c)

☐

☐ ⟶ simple sugars

Q2   Choose from the words below to complete the table showing where **amylase**, **protease**, **lipase** and **bile** are made. You may use some words more than once and you might not need some of them.

pancreas   liver   salivary glands   small intestine

large intestine   stomach   gall bladder   kidneys

Amylase	Protease	Lipase	Bile

Q3 a)   Circle the correct words to complete this passage about bile.

> Bile is stored in the **gall bladder** / **pancreas** before being released into the **liver** / **small intestine**. Bile **acidifies** / **neutralises** the material from the stomach which provides the optimum pH for the **enzymes** / **microorganisms** in the rest of the digestive system to work. Bile breaks **fat** / **glycerol** into smaller droplets.

b)   Explain how emulsification helps digestion.

....

....

Finest emulsion

Biology 2(ii) — Enzymes and Homeostasis

The Digestive System

Q1   Fill in the boxes to label this diagram of the human **digestive system**.

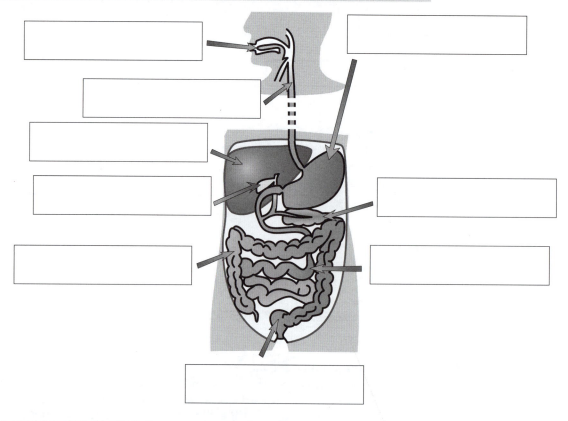

Q2   Number the boxes 1 to 5 to show the **order** that food passes through these parts of the **digestive system**.

- [ ] rectum
- [ ] stomach
- [ ] mouth
- [ ] large intestine
- [ ] small intestine

Q3   Describe the role of each of the following in digestion:

a)   Salivary glands ....

b)   Gall bladder ....

c)   Pancreas ....

d)   Liver ....

e)   Large intestine..

Top Tips: This stuff is pretty easy so it shouldn't take you long to learn. The trickiest bits are probably the roles of the liver and pancreas — make sure you've got those clear in your head.

Biology 2(ii) — Enzymes and Homeostasis

Uses of Enzymes

Q1 **Enzymes** are often used in industrial processes to alter foods. Explain how enzymes can be used in making:

a) **baby foods**

....

....

b) **'slimming' foods**

....

....

....

Q2 The diagram shows two types of **washing powder**.

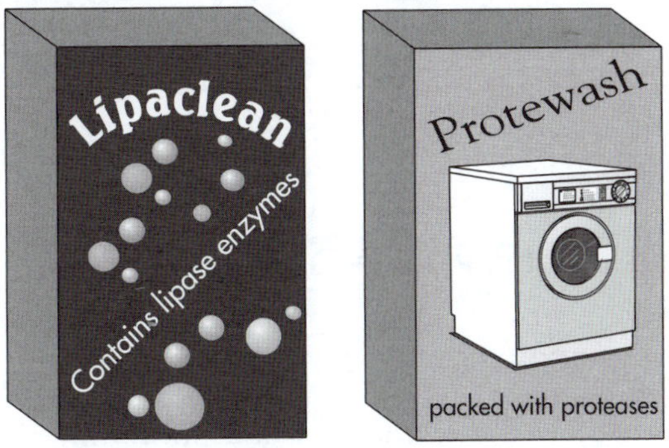

Lipaclean
Contains lipase enzymes

Protewash
packed with proteases

a) Which of the two washing powders would you recommend to someone who has dripped butter on their shirt? Explain your answer.

....

b) Why are some people unable to use washing powders like these?

....

Q3 **Enzymes** are often used to speed up reactions in **industrial processes**.

a) Name two conditions that need to be carefully controlled for the enzymes to work efficiently.

1. ....

2. ....

b) How can enzymes be kept in place during industrial reactions?

....

Homeostasis

Q1   Define the word 'homeostasis'.

....

Q2 a)   Name **four** things that the body has to keep at a **constant** level.

1. ....   2. ....

3. ....   4. ....

b)   Name **two** waste products that have to be removed from the body.

1. ....   2. ....

Q3 a)   Why does the human body need to be kept at around **37 °C**?

....

....

b)   Explain how your body **monitors** its internal temperature.

....

....

....

Q4   Fill in this table describing how different parts of the body help to bring your body temperature back to normal if you get **too hot** or **too cold**. One has been done for you.

	Too hot	Too cold
hair	Hairs lie down flat	
sweat glands		
blood vessels		
muscles		

The Kidneys and Homeostasis

Q1   The kidneys **filter** the **blood**. Label this diagram of the kidneys and the urinary system.

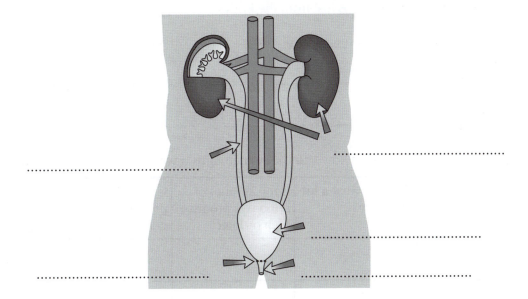

Q2   Tick the correct boxes to show whether these sentences are **true** or **false**.

		True	False
a)	The kidneys make urea.	☐	☐
b)	Breaking down excess amino acids produces urea.	☐	☐
c)	The liver makes urea.	☐	☐
d)	The kidneys monitor blood temperature.	☐	☐
e)	The bladder stores urine.	☐	☐

Q3   One of the kidney's roles is to adjust the **ion content** of the **blood**.

a) Where do the ions in the body come from?

....

b) What would happen if the ion content of the blood wasn't controlled?

....

c) Excess ions are removed from the blood by the kidneys.
   How else can ions be lost from the body?

....

The Kidneys and Homeostasis

Q4 The kidneys are involved in the control of the body's **water levels**.

a) Name three ways that water is lost from the body.

1. ....

2. ....

3. ....

b) Complete the table showing how your body maintains a water balance on hot and cold days.

	Do you sweat **a lot** or **a little**?	Is the amount of urine you produce **high** or **low**?	Is the urine you produce **more** or **less** concentrated?
Hot Day			
Cold Day			

c) Sheona ran 25 km. Afterwards she didn't urinate for six hours. When Sheona did urinate, her urine was a very dark colour. Explain why this happened.

....

....

....

Q5 Unfortunately, some people suffer from **kidney failure**. If someone's kidneys fail they may be given a **kidney transplant**, or they can use a **dialysis machine**. A dialysis machine does the job of the kidneys and filters the blood.

a) What substances would you expect a dialysis machine to remove from the blood?

....

b) Suggest a reason why people with kidney failure are often advised to eat low-salt diets.

....

....

Top Tips: Kidneys do loads of important jobs and that's why kidney failure is so dangerous. You can live with only one kidney and so it is possible for some people with kidney failure to receive a donated kidney from a member of their family.

Controlling Blood Sugar

Q1   Most people's **blood sugar** levels are controlled by **homeostasis**.

a)   Where does the **sugar** in your blood come from?

....

b)   Name the **two** main **organs** that are involved in the control of blood sugar levels.

....

c)   Name **one hormone** that is involved in the regulation of blood sugar levels.

....

Q2   Complete the flow chart to show what happens when **glucose** levels in the blood get too **high**.

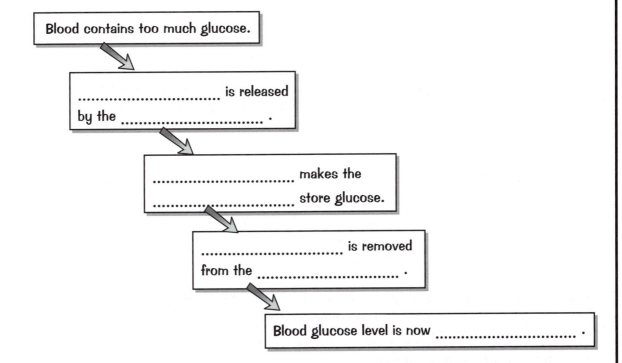

Blood contains too much glucose.

.... is released by the ....

.... makes the .... store glucose.

.... is removed from the ....

Blood glucose level is now ....

Q3   Deepa doesn't eat anything for lunch because she is busy. At **3pm** she has two biscuits and by **6pm** she is so hungry that for tea she eats a plate of pasta and six slices of toast with jam. Sketch a **line graph** showing Deepa's blood sugar levels from **12pm** to **8pm** on the axes below.

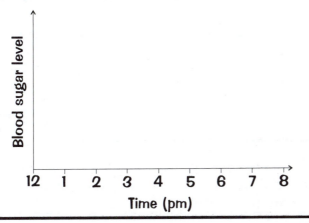

Biology 2(ii) — Enzymes and Homeostasis

Controlling Blood Sugar

Q4   Approximately **1.8 million** people in the UK have **diabetes**.

a)   Explain what type 1 diabetes is.

....

b)   How can diabetics **monitor** their blood sugar levels?

....

Q5   Ruby and Paul both have diabetes, so they need to **monitor** and **control** their glucose levels carefully.

a)   Describe two ways that diabetics can **control** their blood sugar levels.

1. ....

2. ....

b)   Ruby injects insulin just before she is about to eat a big meal. However, she has to go out at short notice and doesn't get time to eat. A few hours later, Ruby faints. Explain why this happens.

....

....

....

....

c)   One evening Paul goes out for a meal. He has forgotten to inject any insulin, and eats a large meal including a sugary desert. A few hours after the meal Paul collapses and has to be taken to hospital for treatment.

i)   Explain why Paul collapsed.

....

....

ii) What treatment would you expect Paul to be given when he arrives at hospital?

....

Top Tips: Although diabetes is a serious disease, many diabetics are able to control their blood sugar levels and carry on with normal lives. Sir Steve Redgrave even won a gold medal at the Olympics after he had been diagnosed with type 1 diabetes.

Insulin and Diabetes

Q1 Tick the correct boxes to show whether these sentences are true or false.   **True False**

a) Insulin is often taken as a tablet. ☐ ☐

b) Needle-free devices can deliver insulin. ☐ ☐

c) When diabetics use insulin they can eat as much food as they like. ☐ ☐

d) The livers of diabetic people have stopped making insulin. ☐ ☐

e) Blood glucose levels can vary a lot without causing a problem. ☐ ☐

Q2 During the 19th century **Banting** and **Best** researched **diabetes** by experimenting on dogs. In some of their experiments they injected an extract into diabetic dogs.

a) Where did they get the extract from?

....

b) When they injected the extract into a diabetic dog, its blood sugar level changed. The changes are shown in the graph below.

i) Describe the effect of the extract.

....

ii) Which hormone did the extract contain? ....

Q3 Since Banting and Best's original research there have been a lot of developments in the treatment of diabetes. Describe the **improvements** that have been made in these areas:

a) The source of the insulin used by diabetics.

....

....

b) The way diabetics take their insulin.

....

....

Insulin and Diabetes

Q4 Injecting insulin can be **painful** and **time-consuming**.

a) What **surgical** treatment can be used to cure type 1 diabetes?

....

b) Describe some of the **problems** with the treatment you have named.

....

....

c) Scientists are constantly researching new treatments and cures for diabetes.
Name **two** treatments that are currently in development.

1. ....

2. ....

Q5 Read this extract about a woman who has diabetes then answer the questions that follow.

Linda is 53, and she's just been diagnosed with Type 2 diabetes. This means that her body doesn't produce enough insulin, or the cells in her body are not reacting normally to the insulin. But Linda's certainly not alone. About 1.5 million people in the UK are known to have the condition, and the numbers are growing. Type 2 diabetes tends to run in families, but it's also strongly linked to obesity — which is an increasing problem in the UK.

If it's not treated, diabetes can lead to other serious medical problems, such as heart disease, strokes or angina. It can also cause poor circulation, which increases the risk of blindness and other eye problems, as well as nerve damage in the hands and feet. Foot ulcers are a common problem for people with diabetes. To ensure that such complications are spotted early and treated effectively, we may need to train more specialist nurses, as well as more chiropodists (foot specialists) and doctors.

The good news for Linda, and many others, is that Type 2 diabetes can often be controlled by diet alone, without the need for insulin injections. Linda's been advised to lose weight, and to start taking regular exercise — "Thirty minutes, at least three times a week, the doctor said." She's also been to see a dietician — "He said I should be eating regular healthy meals, and I've got to cut down on alcohol." Linda pulls a face as she says this, but then grins — "at least I don't smoke, so they can't tell me off about that."

Insulin and Diabetes

a) Circle the actions that Linda has been advised to do to help control her diabetes.

Exercise more   Take tablets   Drink more water   Give up smoking

Inject insulin   Eat healthy food

Drink less alcohol

b) Tick the correct boxes to show whether these sentences are true or false.

True   **False**

i) Diabetes is an increasing problem in the UK. ☐ ☐

ii) Type 2 diabetes is linked to obesity. ☐ ☐

iii) Diabetes does not have a genetic link. ☐ ☐

iv) All diabetics need to inject insulin. ☐ ☐

v) Smoking is the biggest cause of diabetes. ☐ ☐

c) Diabetes can lead to cardiovascular problems such as poor circulation.

i) List the problems that poor circulation can cause in diabetics.

....

....

ii) Why does the extract say that more chiropodists might need to be trained?

....

....

....

d) Linda's husband thinks that her condition isn't very serious because she hasn't been given insulin. Why is Linda's husband wrong?

....

....

Think about the health problems associated with diabetes.

....

....

Mixed Questions — Biology 2(ii)

Q1 a) Name the process which provides energy for movement.

....

b) Give **two products** of this process, other than energy.

....

Q2 The lungs are involved in homeostasis. They excrete carbon dioxide.

Name **one other organ** involved in homeostasis which excretes waste(s) from the body, and name the waste(s) that it removes.

....

....

Q3 Below is a body temperature chart used in a nurses' training pack.

a) Does the chart show the effect of hypothermia or hyperthermia? ....

b) At what temperature does loss of consciousness occur, according to the chart? .... °C

c) It is unusual for internal body temperature to vary from the norm, unless it is exposed to extreme external conditions. Explain how the following help to maintain a **constant internal temperature**:

i) Blood vessels near the surface of the skin **dilating** and **constricting**.

....

....

....

....

ii) Raising hairs.

....

iii) Sweating.

....

Biology 2(ii) — Enzymes and Homeostasis

Mixed Questions — Biology 2(ii)

Q4 a) Which **enzyme** is responsible for the digestion of fats?

....

b) Name a **domestic product** which uses fat-digesting enzymes.

....

c) Enzymes are sometimes used in industry. Give **two advantages** of using enzymes in industrial processes.

1. ....

2. ....

Q5 The diagram below shows how blood sugar level is controlled in humans.

a) Why do your cells need a continual supply of glucose?

....

b) Name "organ A" in the diagram above.

....

c) Excess glucose is removed from your blood and stored in the liver and muscles.

i) Which hormone brings about the removal of glucose?

....

ii) Some people have diabetes (type 1) and cannot produce this hormone. Explain how diabetes is **controlled** and why it **cannot be cured**.

....

....

....

....

....

Biology 2(iii) — Genetics

DNA

Q1 DNA contains all the **instructions** to make an living organism.

a) What does DNA stand for? ....

b) Fill in the blanks in the paragraph using words from the list below.

cells	chromosomes	cytoplasm	gene	amino acids	section	protein	fat

DNA is found in the nucleus of animal and plant .... in molecules

called .... A gene is a .... of DNA. Each gene

contains instructions for the cell to make a specific ....· Cells make

proteins by connecting .... together in a particular order.

c) How many amino acids are used to make proteins in the human body? ....

d) Is everyone's DNA unique? Explain your answer.

....

Q2 **Genetic fingerprinting** is a way of comparing people's DNA — it's useful in forensic science. Put these following stages of DNA fingerprinting into the correct order.

Compare the unique patterns of DNA.

Separate the sections of DNA.

Collect the sample for DNA testing.

Cut the DNA into small sections.

1. ....

2. ....

3. ....

4. ....

Q3 A national **genetic database** would allow everyone's unique pattern of DNA to be saved on file.

a) Give one use of a national genetic database.

....

b) Give one drawback of a national genetic database.

....

DNA

Q4 A thoroughbred horse breeder has collected DNA samples from each of her horses. Her **new foal's DNA** is **sample 1**. Study the **DNA profiles** and complete the table showing which horses are the **foal's parents**.

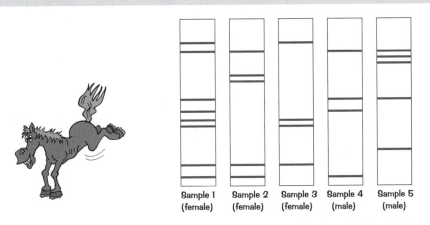

	Foal	Mother	Father
DNA sample	Sample 1		

Q5 The following **DNA samples** are being used in a **murder investigation**. The DNA samples are from the victim, three suspects and some blood which was found on the victim's shirt.

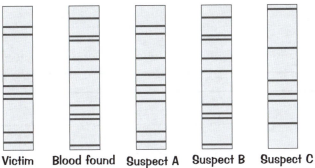

a) Which two individuals are likely to be **related** to each other? Explain your choice.

....

b) Who is the most likely suspect based on the DNA evidence? ....

c) How do you know?

....

d) Can this suspect be accused of murder beyond all doubt?

....

....

Biology 2(iii) — Genetics

Cell Division — Mitosis

Q1   Decide whether the following statements are **true** or **false**.

True False

a)   There are 46 chromosomes in most of your body cells.

b)   There are 20 pairs of chromosomes in a human cheek cell.

c)   Chromosomes are found in the cytoplasm of a cell.

d)   Before a cell divides by mitosis, it duplicates its DNA.

e)   Mitosis is where a cell splits to create two genetically identical copies.

f)   Mitosis produces new cells to replace those which are damaged.

g)   We need mitosis to grow.

Q2   The following diagram shows the different stages of **mitosis**.
Write a short description to explain each stage.

a) ....

b) ....

c) ....
....

d) ....
....

e) ....

Q3   Complete the following passage using the words below.

runners   strawberry   variation   asexual   reproduce   genes

Some organisms use mitosis to .... For example, ...

plants produce .... this way, which become new plants. This is known as

.... reproduction. The offspring have exactly the same

.... as the parent, which means there's no genetic ....

Cell Division — Meiosis

Q1 Tick the boxes below to show which statements are true of **mitosis**, **meiosis** or **both**.

	Mitosis	Meiosis
a) Halves the number of chromosomes.	☐	☐
b) Chromosomes line up in the centre of the cell.	☐	☐
c) Forms cells that are genetically different.	☐	☐
d) In humans, it only happens in the reproductive organs.	☐	☐

Q2 Draw lines to match the descriptions of the stage of **meiosis** to the right diagram below.

a)

b)

c)

d)

e)

The pairs are pulled apart, mixing up the mother and father's chromosomes into the new cells. This creates genetic variation.

Before the cell starts to divide it duplicates its DNA to produce an exact copy.

There are now 4 gametes, each containing half the original number of chromosomes.

For the first meiotic division the chromosomes line up in their pairs across the centre of the cell.

The chromosomes line up across the centre of the nucleus ready for the second division, and the left and right arms are pulled apart.

Q3 During sexual reproduction, two **gametes** combine to form a new individual.

a) What are gametes? ....

b) Explain why gametes have half the usual number of chromosomes.

....

....

c) Explain how we get genetic variation in meiotic cell division.

....

....

Top Tips: It's easy to get confused between mitosis and meiosis. Mitosis occurs in asexual reproduction and makes clones. Meiosis is for sexual reproduction and creates sex cells.

94

Stem Cells

Q1 The following terms are related to **stem cells**. Explain what each term means.

a) specialised cells ....

b) differentiation ....

c) undifferentiated cells ....

Q2 How are **embryonic** stem cells different from **adult** stem cells?

....

....

....

Q3 Describe a way that stem cells are already used in medicine.

....

....

....

Q4 In the future, **embryonic stem cells** might be used to replace faulty cells in sick people. Match the problems below to the potential cures which could be made with stem cells.

diabetes	heart muscle cells
paralysis	insulin-producing cells
heart disease	brain cells
Alzheimer's	nerve cells

Q5 People have **different opinions** when it comes to **stem cell research**.

a) Give one argument **in favour** of stem cell research.

....

....

b) Give one argument **against** stem cell research.

....

....

X and Y Chromosomes

Q1 Tick the boxes to show whether each statement is **true** or **false**.

		True	False
a)	Women have two X chromosomes. Men have an X and a Y chromosome.	☐	☐
b)	There is a 75% chance that a couple's first child will be a girl.	☐	☐
c)	Sperm cells (male gametes) can carry an X or a Y chromosome.	☐	☐
d)	If you have 4 children, you will always get 2 boys and 2 girls.	☐	☐

Q2 Here is a genetic diagram showing the inheritance of **sex chromosomes** in humans.

a) Complete the diagram to show the combinations of chromosomes in the offspring.

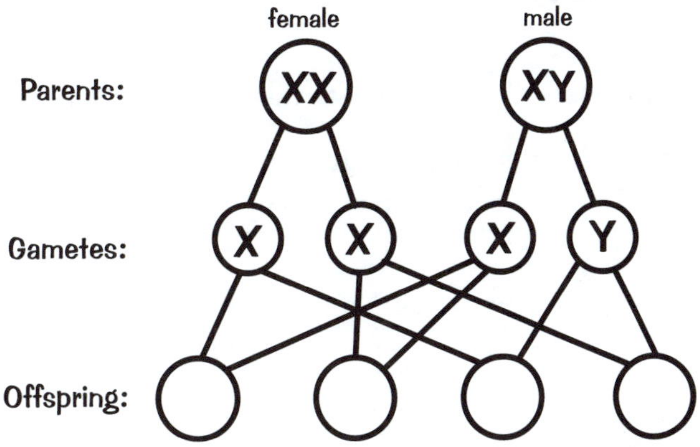

female   male

Parents: XX   XY

Gametes: X   X   X   Y

Offspring: ○   ○   ○   ○

b) A woman becomes pregnant. What is the probability that the embryo is **male**?

....

Q3 **Birds** have sex chromosomes called **Z** and **W** (just like humans have X and Y). In birds, those with **two Z chromosomes** are **male**.

a) What are the female bird's sex chromosomes?

....

b) Complete the genetic diagram below to show the possible combination of gametes in bird reproduction.

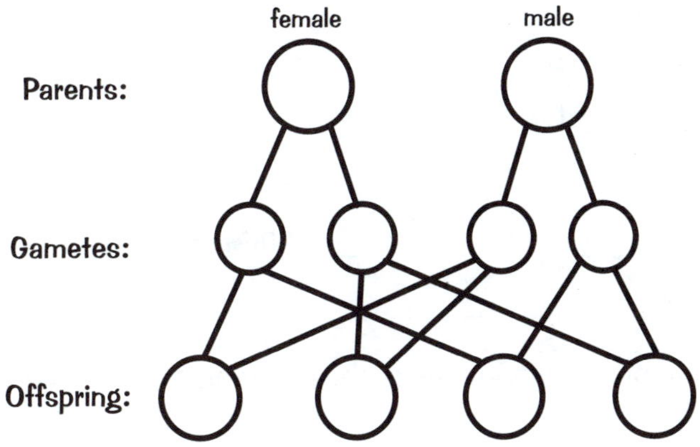

female   male

Parents: ○   ○

Gametes: ○   ○   ○   ○

Offspring: ○   ○   ○   ○

The Work of Mendel

Q1   Use words from the following list to complete the paragraph below.

leaf   genetics   monk   double-glazing salesman   1866   viruses

physicist   characteristics   1980   generation   bulbs

Gregor Mendel was a .... Mendel observed plants in his garden. He realised that .... in plants are passed on from one .... to the next. He published his findings in .... Mendel is regarded by many people as the father of modern ....

Q2   After observing pea plants, Mendel came up with the term 'hereditary unit'.

a)   Explain what Mendel meant by 'hereditary unit'.

....

....

....

b)   Mendel said that some hereditary units were **dominant** and some were **recessive**.
If an organism has both the dominant and the recessive hereditary units for a characteristic, which is expressed?

....

Q3   Mendel crossed different combinations of **tall** and **dwarf** pea plants.

a)   Complete the genetic diagrams below showing crossings of different pea plants.
T represents the dominant allele for **tall plants** and **t** represents the recessive allele for **dwarf plants**.

Cross 1

tall   dwarf

Parents: (TT) (tt)

(T) (T) (t) (t)

Offspring: (Tt) (Tt) ( ) ( )

tall   tall   ....

Cross 2

tall   tall

Parents: (Tt) (Tt)

( ) ( ) ( ) ( )

Offspring: ( ) ( ) ( ) ( )

....

b)   In **cross 2**, what is the probability of one of the offspring plants being tall?

....

Genetic Diagrams

Q1 What is an **allele**?

....

Q2 Wilma the cat carries a **recessive** allele for **light-brown** hair and a **dominant** allele for **black** hair.

a) What colour hair does Wilma have?

....

b) In a genetic diagram, the alleles for hair colour are called **H** and **h**. Which is the **recessive** allele?

....

Q3 A type of fly usually has **red** eyes. However, there are a small number of white-eyed flies. Having **white** eyes is a **recessive** characteristic.

a) Complete the following sentences with either '**red eyes**' or '**white eyes**'.

i) **R** is the allele for ....

ii) **r** is the allele for ....

iii) Flies with alleles **RR** or **Rr** will have ....

iv) Flies with the alleles **rr** will have ....

b) Two flies have the alleles **Rr**. They fall in love and get it on.

i) Complete this genetic diagram to show the alleles of the possible offspring. One's been done for you.

parent's alleles

	R	r
R	RR	
r		

parent's alleles

Read up and across to work out what combination of alleles should be in each box.

ii) What is the probability that one of the flies' offspring will have white eyes?

....

iii) The flies have 96 offspring. How many of the offspring are **likely** to have **red eyes**?

....

Genetic Diagrams

Q4 Seeds of pea plants can be **smooth** or **wrinkled**. The allele for smooth seeds (**S**) is dominant. The allele for wrinkled seeds (**s**) is recessive.

a) The diagrams below shows a cross between a thoroughbred pea plant with smooth seeds (genetic type **SS**) and a thoroughbred pea plant with wrinkled seeds (genetic type **ss**).

Complete the genetic diagram.

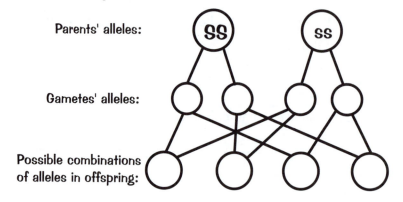

Parents' alleles:

Gametes' alleles:

Possible combinations
of alleles in offspring:

b) In this cross, what is the probability of one offspring producing wrinkled seeds? Tick the correct option.

- [ ] 100% chance of producing wrinkled seeds
- [ ] 50% chance of producing wrinkled seeds
- [ ] 25% chance of producing wrinkled seeds
- [ ] 0% chance of producing wrinkled seeds

Pictures of peas are very dull.
So here's a picture of Elvis instead.

c) Two hybrid pea plants (**Ss**) are interbred.
Complete the genetic diagram to show the possible combinations of alleles in the offspring.

	parent's alleles	
	S	**s**
S		
s		

(left axis label: **parent's alleles**)

d) Is the following statement **true** or **false**? Tick the correct box.

"Mrs Maguire crosses two pea plants with the alleles Ss. If she gets 12 new seedlings as a result, it's most likely that 3 of the seedlings will produce wrinkled seeds."

True False
[ ] [ ]

Top Tips: Genetic diagrams look like alphabet spaghetti at first — but they're OK really. They're useful for working out the possible combinations of alleles that offspring can get from their parents — and the probability of each combination.

Genetic Disorders

Q1 **Cystic fibrosis** is a **genetic disorder** which affects cell membranes. It is caused by a **recessive** allele, which can be passed on from parents to their children.

a) Complete the following genetic diagram showing the inheritance of cystic fibrosis. The recessive allele for cystic fibrosis is **f**, and the dominant allele is **F**.

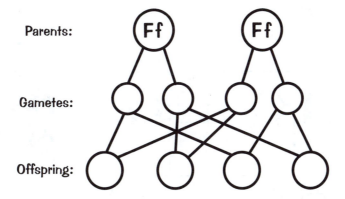

b) i) In the above genetic diagram, what is the probability of a child having cystic fibrosis?

....

ii) In the above genetic diagram, what is the probability of a child being a **carrier** of the cystic fibrosis allele (but not having the disease)?

....

Q2 Huntington's disease is a genetic disorder caused by a **dominant** allele. Below is a genetic diagram for the inheritance of Huntington's disease.

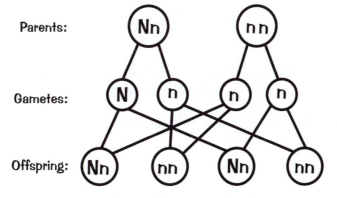

a) Two adults with the alleles Nn and nn decide to have children. What is the probability of their first child inheriting the allele for Huntington's disease?

....

b) Symptoms of Huntington's disease may not appear until a person is over 40 years old. Why does this increase the chance of the disease being passed on?

....

....

Genetic Disorders

Q3   Genetic disorders can be inherited. Huntington's disease has been passed on through the family shown in the diagram below:

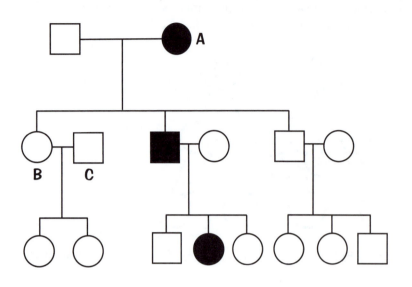

Key

☐ male without the allele for Huntington's disease

◯ female without the allele for Huntington's disease

■ male with allele for Huntington's disease

● female with allele for Huntington's disease

Remember that Huntington's disease is caused by a dominant allele.

a)   Will person A develop Huntington's disease at some point in their life?

....

b)   Is it possible that the couple B and C could have a child with the allele for Huntington's disease? Explain your answer.

....

....

Q4   During in vitro fertilisation (IVF) a cell can be removed from an embryo and screened for genetic disorders like Huntington's disease. If a faulty allele is present, the embryo is destroyed.

a)   Explain why some people think embryo screening is a **bad** thing.

....

....

....

b)   Explain why some people think embryo screening is a **good** thing.

....

....

....

More Genetic Diagrams

Q1 Sickle cell anaemia is a genetic disorder which affects the shape of red blood cells. It is caused by a **recessive** allele. If both parents are **carriers** of the recessive allele then their children are most likely to show a **1 : 2 : 1 ratio** of the different combinations of alleles (**normal : carrier : sufferer**).

A scientist does a survey of **100 children** whose **parents** are **both carriers** of the sickle cell anaemia allele (i.e. the parents all have the alleles **Aa**). Complete the table below to show how many children in the survey are likely to have each gene type.

Gene type:	AA (normal)	Aa (carrier)	aa (sufferer)
Probable number of children:			

Q2 An allele for the colour grey (**G**) in mice is dominant over the allele for the colour white (**g**). A hybrid grey mouse (**Gg**) was bred with a thoroughbred white mouse (**gg**).

a) Complete the genetic diagram below to show the potential combinations of alleles in the offspring of the two mice.

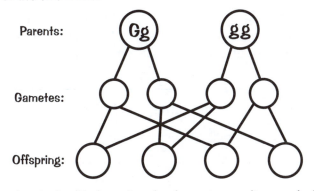

Parents:

Gametes:

Offspring:

'Hybrid' = an organism which has two different alleles for the same characteristic, e.g. Hh.
Thoroughbred = an organism which has two identical alleles for a characteristic, e.g. HH or hh.

b) What is the likely ratio of colours in any litters of offspring (grey : white)?

....

c) If the mice had 12 babies, how many would there be **likely** to be of each colour?

....

Q3 Sally is investigating the inheritance of **flower colours**. She knows that the allele for the colour **red** is **dominant** over the allele for the colour **white**.

Sally has two **genetically identical** plants, one with **red** flowers and one with **white** flowers. Suggest how Sally can find out whether the plant with red flowers is thoroughbred red (**RR**) or hybrid red (**Rr**).

....

....

....

....

Extract on Embryo Screening

Q1   Read this passage about embryo screening.

> Embryo screening already happens in the UK for genetic disorders like Huntington's disease. A genetic test can be done during IVF treatment — so that doctors can select a healthy embryo to implant in the mother. The other embryos are discarded.
>
> At the moment, regulations say that embryo screening is only allowed when there is "a significant risk of a serious genetic condition being present in the embryo." In other words, when the person carrying the faulty allele is certain (or almost certain) to get the disorder, and the disorder is serious. So screening for short-sightedness wouldn't be allowed, even if we knew that people with a faulty allele would definitely become short-sighted.
>
> Medical technology has made it possible to test for several genes that are linked to very serious illnesses, e.g. cancers. But, in many cases, the faulty allele isn't certain to cause cancer — it increases the risk, sometimes by a lot, but sometimes just slightly. So, at the moment, screening for alleles like this isn't allowed. Many people say this is right. Some kinds of cancer can be treated very successfully, so perhaps it's wrong to destroy embryos that might never become ill anyway — and which have a good chance of recovery if they do.
>
> One alternative to embryo screening is prenatal testing. This means that the parents conceive naturally and have the fetus tested as it's developing in the mother's womb. If the baby is carrying a faulty allele, the mother may then choose to have an abortion. For some people, this raises other ethical concerns.

a) Could embryos be screened for colour-blindness under the current regulations? Explain your answer.

....

....

b) Cancer is a serious illness that kills thousands of people each year in the UK. Why is cancer not included in embryo screening?

....

....

....

....

....

c) Describe an alternative to embryo screening.

....

....

Top Tips: Extracts can be a bit scary — all that scientific sc016formation in a big wodge. Try reading the extract once, then reading the questions and then reading the extract again, underlining any useful bits. The extract's there to help you with the questions — so use it.

Mixed Questions — Biology 2(iii)

Q1 a) What unique characteristic do **stem cells** have which ordinary body cells don't have?

....

b) Suggest why **embryos** contain many stem cells.

....

....

c) Scientists have experimented with growing stem cells in different conditions.
What is the name of the process by which stem cells **divide** for growth?

....

d) Although there is potential for medical breakthroughs, some people disagree with stem cell research on ethical grounds. Describe one **ethical issue** surrounding stem cell research.

....

....

Q2 In one of Gregor Mendel's experiments, he crossed thoroughbred purple-flowered pea plants with thoroughbred white-flowered plants. The **first generation** of offspring were **all purple-flowered**.

a) In Mendel's experiment, which characteristic is recessive?

....

b) Using the symbols **F** and **f** to represent the alleles for **purple** and **white**, write down the combination of alleles (genetic make-up) of each of the following:

i) the original purple-flowered parent plant

....

ii) the original white-flowered parent plant

....

iii) the first generation of purple-flowered offspring

....

c) Modern genetics experiments are often done with fruit flies.
Suggest an **advantage** of using fruit flies rather than pea plants.

....

....

Mixed Questions — Biology 2(iii)

Q3   **Albinism** is a genetic condition. Affected people, called albinos, lack any skin pigmentation. A couple, neither of whom is albino, have a child who is an albino.

Is the allele for albinism dominant or recessive? Explain your answer.

....

....

....

Q4   Two grey rabbits are mated, and eight offspring are produced. Five of the offspring have grey fur, and three have white fur. The allele for grey fur (**G**) is dominant. The allele for white fur (**g**) is recessive. The **parent rabbits** are both **hybrid** with the alleles **Gg**.

a)   Draw a **genetic cross diagram** in the space below, to show the **probability** of each combination of alleles occurring in the offspring of the rabbits.

b) i)   What is the predicted ratio of grey to white rabbits in the offspring?

....

ii)   Explain why the actual ratio of colours in the offspring is not exactly the same as this.

....

....

c)   If two white rabbits are mated together, what proportion of their offspring will be white? Explain your answer.

....

....

....

Gas and Solute Exchange

Q1 Substances move through partially permeable membranes by **three** processes.

a) Place a cross in the correct boxes to identify the features of each process.

Feature	Diffusion	Osmosis	Active transport
Substances move from areas of higher concentration to areas of lower concentration			
Requires energy			

b) What is the main difference between diffusion and osmosis?

....

Q2 A diagram of a cross-section through part of a **leaf** is shown.

a) Suggest what substance is represented by each of the letters shown on the diagram.

A ....

B ....

C ....

b) By what process do all these substances enter and leave the leaf? ....

c) How is the amount of these substances that enter and leave the leaf controlled?

....

....

d) State two places where gaseous exchange takes place in a leaf.

1. ....

2. ....

e) Suggest one advantage of leaves having a flattened shape.

....

Q3 a) Indicate whether each of the following statements is **true** or **false**.

True   False

i) Leaves are adapted to aid the diffusion of gases. ☐ ☐

ii) Guard cells are important for controlling water loss from leaves. ☐ ☐

iii) In dry conditions leaf stomata are likely to be open. ☐ ☐

iv) Air spaces in leaves reduce the surface area for gas exchange. ☐ ☐

v) Plants are likely to wilt when they lose more water than is replaced. ☐ ☐

b) Plants lose water vapour to the surroundings by diffusion.
What name is given to the diffusion of water vapour from plants? ....

Gas and Solute Exchange

Q4 Mary wanted to compare **water loss** from two plants — a **geranium** and a **cactus**. She added some water to each plant, then sealed the base in a plastic bag to prevent water from escaping from the base. She weighed the plants at the start of the investigation and again two days later.

a) Suggest one way Mary could ensure that this is a **fair test**.

....

b) Explain why it is important the bags were properly sealed around the base of each plant.

....

c) Assuming both plants have the same total surface area, which plant would you expect to have lost **less** water? Explain your answer.

....

....

Q5 Lucy was investigating the water loss from basil plants in **different conditions**. She used twelve plants, three plants in each of the four different conditions. The plants were weighed before and after the experiment. Lucy calculated the % change in the mass and recorded her results in a table.

a) Calculate the average % change in plant mass for the three plants in each of the conditions and write the results in the table.

Plant	In a room (% change in mass)	Next to a fan (% change in mass)	By a lamp (% change in mass)	Next to a fan and by a lamp (% change in mass)
1	5	8	10	13
2	5	9	11	15
3	4	11	9	13
Average				

b) Which conditions caused the greatest water loss? Circle the correct answer.

  in a room   next to a fan   by a lamp   next to a fan and by a lamp

c) Suggest why Lucy used **three** plants in each of the conditions shown.

....

d) Lucy then covered the lower surfaces of the leaves with **petroleum jelly**. How would this affect the rate of water loss from the leaves?

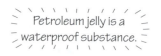
Petroleum jelly is a waterproof substance.

....

e) The water loss from a plant in a hot, dry day is shown on the graph. Sketch the graph you would expect for the same plant on a **cold, wet** day.

(Graph: Total water loss (g) on y-axis, Time (hours) on x-axis, curve labelled "Hot, dry day")

f) Predict what would happen to a plant if the rate of transpiration was higher than the rate of water supplied to the plant. ....

The Breathing System

Q1   **Define** the processes listed below and state **where** in the human body each of the processes occur.

a)   i)   **Respiration**

....

ii)   It occurs in ....

b)   i)   **Breathing**

....

ii)   It occurs in ....

Q2 a)   On the diagram show the positions of the following structures by placing the correct letter in the correct box:

A   alveoli

B   bronchus

C   trachea

D   bronchiole

b)   Complete the passages below using the words given.   Each word may be used more than once.

out	flattens	drawn into	in	diaphragm	up
increase	decreases	down	intercostal	fall
forced out of	rises	volume	relax	ribcage

When we breathe .... the .... muscles and the .... contract. This means the diaphragm .... and the ribcage and the sternum move .... and .... This makes the volume of the thorax .... in size, which causes a .... in pressure. Air is then .... the lungs.

Breathing out occurs when the intercostal muscles and the diaphragm .... This means that the .... and sternum move .... and .... As a result the .... of the thorax .... and the pressure ...., meaning that air is .... the lungs.

Q3   **Asthma** is a condition where the air passages **constrict** in response to a stimulus, e.g. pollen or dust. Suggest why people with asthma may have difficulty doing **strenuous exercise**.

....

Biology 3(i) — Life Processes 2

Diffusion Through Cell Membranes

Q1 Parts of the human body are **adapted** to speed up the **rate of diffusion** of various substances.

a) State two parts of the body that are adapted to aid diffusion.

....

b) Name two substances that enter the bloodstream by diffusion.

....

c) Suggest one essential process in the body that requires
the substances you have identified in part b) above. ....

d) Where in the body does this process occur? ....

Q2 The movements of two gases **A** and **B** in an **alveolus** are shown.

a) Add these labels to the diagram: **capillary**,
plasma, **red blood cell**, **alveolus**.

b) Name the two gases that are passing
through the walls of the alveolus.

A ....

B ....

c) Name the **process** by which these gases
travel across the wall of the alveolus.

....

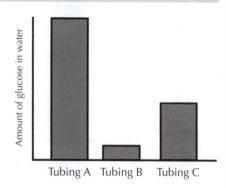

Q3 A piece of **Visking tubing** is often used as a model for the walls of the small intestine. Jenny filled
three pieces of Visking tubing with **starch** solution and different concentrations of the enzyme
amylase, as shown in the diagram. Amylase breaks down starch into smaller **glucose** molecules.

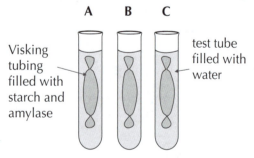

Visking
tubing
filled with
starch and
amylase

test tube
filled with
water

The amount of glucose
sugar present in the
water surrounding the
Visking tubing in each
test tube was measured
after four hours. The
results are shown in the
graph.

a) The three concentrations of amylase added to the Visking
tubing were 0.5 mmol, 2 mmol and 5 mmol. Decide which
concentration of amylase was present in each tubing.

A ....   B ....   C ....

b) Suggest why the water in each test tube was only tested for the presence of **glucose** and not for the
presence of starch.

....

Diffusion Through Cell Membranes

Q4   Some features that help to **speed up** the rate of diffusion in **villi** and **alveoli** are listed below.

a) Place a tick in the correct column to indicate whether each feature is found in a villus, an alveolus or both structures.

Features	Alveolus	Villus	Reason
Thin walls			
Good blood supply			
Moist lining			
Single layer of surface cells			
Large surface area			

b) Indicate **why** each feature is important for diffusion, choosing reason **A**, **B** or **C** below. Write the letter in the table. (Each letter can be used more than once.)

A Makes diffusion faster by maintaining a large concentration difference

B Makes diffusion faster by creating a short distance for particles to diffuse across

C Makes diffusion faster by some other means

Q5   Villi increase the **surface area** of the gut for the uptake of nutrients. Pablo conducted an experiment to investigate the effect of surface area using four **gelatine cubes** of **different sizes**. He placed the cubes in a dish of food dye and measured how quickly they absorbed the dye. His results are shown in the table.

Size (mm)	Surface area (mm²)	Average time for dye uptake (mins)
1 x 1 x 1		1.5
2 x 2 x 2		4.4
5 x 5 x 5		6.2
10 x 10 x 10		16.3

a) Calculate the missing values for **surface area**.

b) Complete these statements by circling the correct word.

i) As the cubes become bigger in size their surface area becomes **bigger** / **smaller**.

ii) As the surface area becomes smaller the rate of dye uptake **increases** / **decreases**.

c) Explain how the results from this experiment show that villi increase the rate of nutrient uptake from the gut.

....

Active Transport

Q1 A diagram of a **specialised plant cell** is shown.

a) Name the type of cell shown. ....

b) What is the main **function** of this type of cell?

....

c) Explain why minerals are **not** usually absorbed from the soil by the process of **diffusion**.

....

d) Explain how these specialised cells absorb minerals from the soil.
Use the words **active transport**, **concentration**, **respiration** and **energy** in your answer.

....

....

Q2 Theo conducted an investigation into how quickly glucose is absorbed from the gut.
Four subjects **fasted** for 12 hours before the investigation began and then were each given a
meal containing a different amount of starch (starch is broken down in the gut into glucose).

a) Suggest why there was a 15 minute time **delay**
between eating the meals that contained
starch and absorption from the gut.

....

....

b) Compare the **initial rate** of glucose
absorption for the four meals. Use evidence
from the graph to support your answer.

....

c) Suggest why the rate of absorption **decreased** after a period of time.

....

d) Which process, **active transport** or **diffusion**, do you think was responsible for the uptake of
glucose in these subjects? Explain your answer.

....

....

Top Tips: Don't forget that active transport uses energy. This energy comes from respiration.
Active transport also happens in the kidney tubules and loads of other places.

Biology 3(i) — Life Processes 2

Active Transport

Q3 Aaron planted two **plants** in his garden. He noticed that one plant didn't grow very well.

a) Suggest a reason that might account for the poor growth of plant A.

....

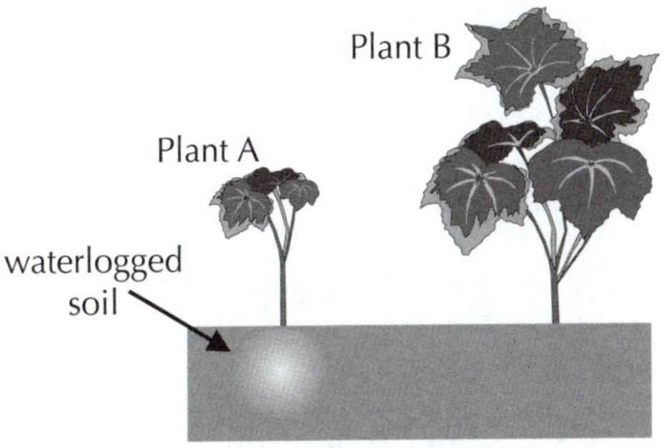

Plant B

Plant A

waterlogged soil

Aerobic respiration needs oxygen.

b) Apart from water, what do plants absorb from the soil that is essential for growth? Name the process responsible for this uptake.

....

....

c) Waterlogged soils contain little **oxygen**. How might this explain poor plant growth? Use the terms **minerals**, **active transport** and **energy** in your answer.

....

....

....

Q4 Two germinating barley seedlings were placed in solutions that contained a known concentration of **potassium ions**, as shown in the diagram. The uptake of potassium ions was measured.

a) State two ways to ensure this is a fair test.

....

....

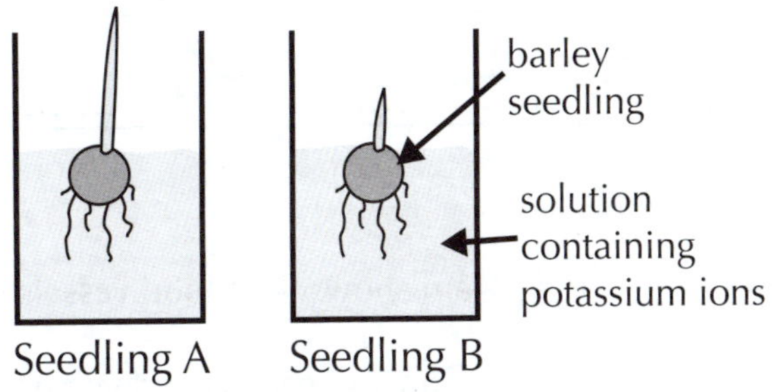

barley seedling

solution containing potassium ions

Seedling A   Seedling B

The graph below shows the uptake of potassium ions by the barley seedlings.

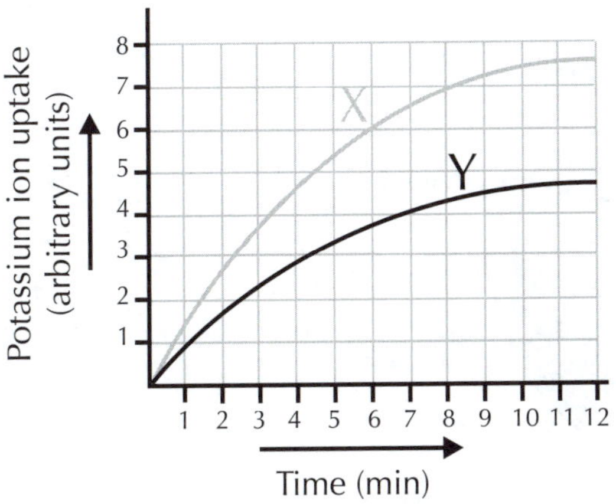

b) Which curve represents seedling **A**? Circle the correct answer.

X   **Y**

Explain how you decided.

....

....

c) What is the potassium ion uptake for seedling A after **10 minutes**?

....

Potassium ion uptake (arbitrary units)

Time (min)

The Circulation System

Q1 State two **functions** of the circulation system. For each function you have given name **two substances** that are **transported**.

Function 1: ....

substances transported: .... and ....

Function 2: ....

substances transported: .... and ....

Q2 a) Draw lines to join the three types of **blood vessel** with their correct description.

Vein		Tiny vessel in contact with body cells
Capillary		Large vessel carrying blood towards the heart
Artery		Large vessel carrying blood away from the heart

b) Put the words below in the boxes to show the correct sequence of **blood flow** around the body. The first one has been done for you. (Each word may be used more than once.)

capillaries   organs   arteries   veins   cells   heart

| Heart | | .... | | .... | | .... |

| .... | | .... | | .... | | .... |

Q3 The diagram shows the **blood vessels** of the **heart**.

Write the name of each blood vessel beside the letters on the diagram.

A ....   B ....

C ....   D ....

Right-hand side   Left-hand side

The Circulation System

Q4   The heart is designed to pump blood around the body.

a)   Explain why the heart is thought of as **two pumps** rather than a single pump.

....

....

b) **i)**   Which side of the heart pumps blood to the **lungs**? ....

      ii) Is the blood on this side oxygenated or deoxygenated?
Circle the correct answer.

            oxygenated   **deoxygenated**

c) **i)**   Which side of the heart pumps blood to the **body**? ....

      ii) Is the blood on this side oxygenated or deoxygenated?
Circle the correct answer.

            oxygenated   **deoxygenated**

d)   Suggest why the left side of the heart is more muscular than the right side.

Think about which side has to pump harder.

....

....

Q5   Blood travels in a **continuous circuit** around the body.

Place in order the parts of the body a red blood cell starting in the gut
will travel through until it leaves the heart to return to the gut.
Each letter can be used more than once.

A   Aorta

B   Pulmonary artery

C   Liver

D   Heart

E   Vena cava

F   Blood vessel to the liver

G   Lungs

H   Pulmonary vein

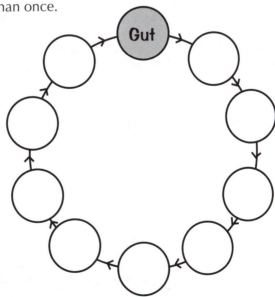

Top Tips: Make sure you understand where the blood goes and what vessels carry it where. Remember that **a**rteries always carry blood **a**way from the heart. Arteries all carry oxygenated blood except for the pulmonary artery — which carries deoxygenated blood to the lungs to get more oxygen.

Blood

Q1 Which of these statements are **true**, and which are **false**? Tick the correct boxes.

True False

a) The function of red blood cells is to fight germs. ☐ ☐

b) White blood cells help to fight infection. ☐ ☐

c) Glucose can be found in the blood. ☐ ☐

d) The liquid part of blood is called urine. ☐ ☐

e) Platelets help seal wounds to prevent blood loss. ☐ ☐

f) Blood is a tissue. ☐ ☐

Tissues are made of groups of similar cells.

Q2 A diagram of a **capillary** is shown.

a) Capillary walls are only **one cell** thick.
How does this feature make them suited to their function?

....

b) Name two **gases** that diffuse through the walls of capillaries.

....

c) Name two other substances that diffuse through the walls of capillaries.

....

Q3 **Red blood cells** carry **oxygen** in the blood.

a) **i)** Name the substance in red blood cells that combines with oxygen. ....

ii) Name the substance created when oxygen joins with this substance. ....

b) Red blood cells are replaced about every 120 days. Approximately
how many times per year are all the red cells in the body replaced? ....

Q4 a) List six things that are carried by **plasma**.

1. ....   4. ....

2. ....   5. ....

3. ....   6. ....

b) For each of the substances
listed in the table, state
where each is travelling
from and **to** in the blood.

Substance	Travelling from	Travelling to
Urea		
Carbon dioxide		
Glucose		

Exercise

Q1   Complete the following sentences by circling the correct answers.

a) During exercise our muscles need more **energy** / **water** to enable them to keep **relaxing** / **contracting**.

b) This means they need a continuous supply of **protein** / **glucose** and **carbon dioxide** / **oxygen**.

c) Glucose is released from stores of **starch** / **glycogen** — the stores are used up **slowly** / **quickly** during exercise.

d) Extra oxygen is obtained by increasing **breathing rate** / **digestion**.

e) The heart rate **speeds up** / **slows down** and the arteries **dilate** / **narrow** to supply blood more **quickly** / **slowly** to the muscles.

f) Eventually the muscles become **tired** / **energised**, particularly when energy is released **with** / **without oxygen**. This is called **anaerobic** / **aerobic** respiration.

Q2   John has to sprint for the bus because he is late.

a) State **two** effects this sudden physical exercise has on John's body. Explain why each change is necessary.

1. ....

2. ....

b) After his initial sprint, John's leg muscles become painful.

i) Suggest what substance is causing this pain. ....

ii) What **process** produces this substance? ....

c) When he gets on the bus he's out of breath. Explain why he continues to breathe deeply for a while.

....

....

....

Q3   Use the words given to complete the word equations for the two types of respiration. Each word can be used more than once.

| carbon dioxide | oxygen | lactic acid | water | glucose | energy |

Aerobic: .... + ... → .... + ... (+ ....)

Anaerobic: .... → .... (+ ....)

Kidneys

Q1 The diagram shows the steps that occur from the entry of blood into the kidneys to the exit of blood from the kidneys. Write the labels A to G in the diagram to show the correct order.

A Wastes such as urea, are carried out of the nephron to the bladder, whilst reabsorbed materials leave the kidneys in the renal vein.

B Small molecules are squeezed into the Bowman's capsule. Large molecules remain in the blood.

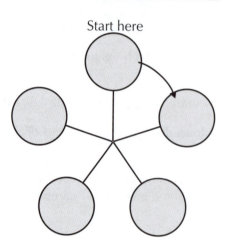

Start here

C Useful products are reabsorbed from the nephron and enter the capillaries.

D Molecules travel from the Bowman's capsule along the nephron.

E Blood enters the kidney through the renal artery.

Q2 The blood entering the kidney contains the following:

    ions   water   proteins   sugar   urea   blood cells

a) List the things that are:

   i) filtered out of the blood ....

   ii) reabsorbed ....

   iii) released in the urine ....

b) Which process is responsible for the **reabsorption** of each substance you have listed above?

....

c) **i)** Name two things that do **not** enter the Bowman's capsule.

....

   ii) Explain why these things are not able to leave the bloodstream.

....

Q3 Three people are tested to see how healthy their kidneys are. Levels of **protein** and **glucose** in their urine are measured. The results are shown in the table.

Which of the three subjects might have kidney damage? Explain how you decided.

....

....

....

Subject	Protein (mg/24 hours)	Glucose (mmol/litre)
1	12	0
2	260	1.0
3	0	0

Kidney Failure

Q1 **Kidney failure** can be treated by dialysis or a kidney transplant. Place a tick in the table to show the features of the two types of treatment.

Feature of treatment	Dialysis	Transplant
High risk of infection		
May create problems among family members		
Long-term, one-off treatment		
Patient can lead a relatively normal life		
Patient must take drugs		
Only one treatment is required		
Patient usually needs to live near a hospital		

Q2 A model of **dialysis** is shown below. No movement of substances has taken place yet.

Blood   Dialysis fluid

○ Red blood cell   membrane
● Protein   ○ Water
▪ Urea   ● Glucose

a) **i)** Which two substances will **not** diffuse across the membrane from the bloodstream into the dialysis fluid.

....

ii) Explain your answer.

....

....

b) Which substance's concentration will increase in the dialysis fluid? ....

c) What do you notice about the concentration of glucose on either side of the membrane? Suggest a reason for this.

....

....

Q3 The graph shows the numbers of kidney transplant patients and numbers of donors in the **UK**.

a) Describe the trend in the number of people on the transplant waiting list.

....

....

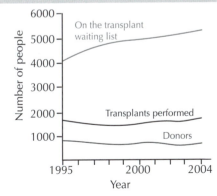

b) What is the general trend for donors and transplants performed compared to the number of people on the transplant waiting list?

....

c) Give **two** sources of kidney donations.

....

Kidney Failure

Q4 One method of treatment for kidney failure is to use **dialysis**. The steps in dialysis are listed. Number the steps in the correct order by writing 1 to 5 in the boxes.

[ ] Excess water, ions and wastes are filtered out of the blood and pass into the dialysis fluid.

[ ] The patient's blood flows into the dialysis machine and between partially permeable membranes.

[ ] Blood is returned to the patient's body using a vein in their arm.

[ ] Dialysis continues until nearly all the waste and excess substances are removed.

[ ] A needle is inserted into a blood vessel in the patient's arm to remove blood.

Q5 The table shows the number of UK patients with **kidney failure** in **2004** and predicted numbers for **2013**.

a) Calculate the number of patients who received a kidney **transplant** in **2004**. Write your answer in the table.

b) Calculate the number of patients who are likely to be receiving **dialysis** in **2013**. Write your answer in the table.

	Year	
	2004	2013
Total number of patients with kidney failure	37 000	68 000
Number receiving dialysis	20 500	
Number that have received a transplant		30 000

c) This table shows the cost of each treatment.

Calculate the amount of money saved per patient when a **transplant** is performed:

Treatment	Average cost per patient (£)
Dialysis	30 000 per year
Transplant	20 000
Anti-rejection drugs	6 500 per year

i) instead of **one** year of **dialysis**.

....

ii) instead of **three** years of **dialysis**.

....

....

Don't forget that transplant patients need drugs to stop organ rejection.

Q6 List three steps that are taken to reduce the chances of **rejection** of a transplanted kidney.

1. ....

2. ....

3. ....

Biology 3(i) — Life Processes 2

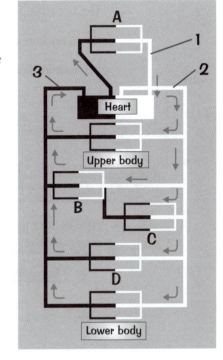

Mixed Questions — Biology 3(i)

Q1 The diagram represents the main features of the **circulation system**.

Deoxygenated blood is represented by black lines, and oxygenated blood by white lines. The arrows show the direction of movement. Using your knowledge and the clues in the diagram, **match** the blood vessels labelled 1 – 3 and the organs labelled A – D to their correct names in the table.

Blood vessels	Number	Organs	Letter
Pulmonary vein		Intestines	
Aorta		Kidneys	
Vena cava		Liver	
		Lungs	

Q2 Neela had to **sprint** for the bus.

a) Describe a **change** that occurred in her circulation system.

....

b) How does this help her to run fast?

....

c) When she got on the bus her legs were **tired** and it took a few minutes for her to **catch her breath**.

i) What **process** was producing the **energy** she needed to contract her leg muscles while running?

....

ii) Write the word equation for this process.

....

iii) Why did she have to **continue breathing hard** after she had stopped running?

....

....

d) Aerobic respiration requires **oxygen** and **glucose**.

i) By what process does oxygen move into the bloodstream in the lungs?

....

ii) How does glucose move into the bloodstream from the gut when there is a low concentration of glucose in the gut?

....

iii) Name two ways in which the **villi** in the small intestine are adapted to absorb glucose quickly.

....

....

Mixed Questions — Biology 3(i)

Q3   Circle the correct words to complete the passage below about the **breathing system**.

"The breathing system takes **air / oxygen** into and out of the body. This

allows **carbon dioxide / oxygen** to pass from the air into the bloodstream,

and **carbon dioxide / oxygen** to pass out of the bloodstream into the air."

Q4   Sentences A to F below are all to do with movements of the thorax
and diaphragm when we **breathe in**, but they have been muddled up.

A The pressure inside the thorax gets less than atmospheric pressure.

B Air is pushed into the lungs from outside to make the pressures equal.

C This causes the diaphragm to flatten and pulls the ribcage upwards.

D The pressure inside the thorax goes down.

E The volume of the thorax increases.

F The diaphragm muscles contract and the muscles between the ribs contract.

Write down the letters to show the correct order.

....

Q5   We each have around 600 million **alveoli** in our lungs.
This ensures that we can get enough oxygen into our
bloodstream and remove the waste carbon dioxide from it.

   a) Describe four ways in which the alveoli are specialised to
maximise gas exchange.

....

....

....

....

   b)   **i)**   Which **cells** in the blood carry the oxygen that has diffused through the alveoli walls?

....

   ii) Which **substance** in the cell combines with the oxygen? ....

   iii) How are the cells **adapted** to carry oxygen?

....

....

Biology 3(i) — Life Processes 2

Mixed Questions — Biology 3(i)

Q6 Part of the blood is a **straw-coloured liquid**.

a) Name this part of the blood. ....

b) Name two substances present in this liquid that are **filtered out** by the kidneys.

....

c) Name a substance that is **reabsorbed** into the capillary network.

....

d) How are **capillaries** adapted to aid the diffusion of substances?

....

....

Q7 Tick the correct box to show whether each statement is **true** or **false**.

		True	False
a)	Kidney failure can be treated by dialysis or a kidney transplant.	☐	☐
b)	Dialysis fluid has a higher concentration of water than the blood.	☐	☐
c)	Substances move from the blood to the dialysis fluid by diffusion.	☐	☐
d)	You can donate one of your kidneys and still function normally.	☐	☐
e)	Patients who receive a kidney must take drugs to suppress their immune system.	☐	☐
f)	Excess proteins cross from the blood into the dialysis fluid.	☐	☐

Q8 The diagram shows a **specialised cell**.

a) Name the cell shown.

....

b) Explain how the cell's **shape** helps it to absorb **water**.

....

c) The cell is exposed to a poison that stops respiration.
Why would this affect the uptake of **minerals** but not the uptake of **water**?

....

....

d) **i)** Water absorbed by the roots is lost through the leaves as vapour.
What process does it escape by and what is the proper name for the process in plants?

....

ii) Under what conditions is water loss at its greatest? ....

iii) Name another gas that escapes out of a leaf. ....

Food and Drink from Microorganisms

Q1 **Lazzaro Spallanzani** was a scientist who tried to **disprove** the idea of **spontaneous generation**. He boiled some broth in a flask, and then sealed the flask. The broth didn't go bad.

a) Why was it necessary to seal the flask? ....

b) The broth only stays fresh if the flask is sealed **before** it cools down. Explain why this is so.

....

c) Spallanzani then opened the flask and left it open for a while. The broth eventually went bad. Explain the purpose of this part of the experiment.

....

Q2 **Louis Pasteur** did an experiment in which he boiled some broth in two different flasks — flasks A and B below. He then allowed the broth to cool.

flask open to air

boiled broth

Flask A   Flask B

a) In which flask did the broth go bad, and why?

....

....

b) Explain why the broth in the other flask did not go bad.

....

c) Explain why, for flask B, Pasteur used a long curved neck instead of sealing the flask with a stopper.

....

Q3 **Cheese** is made using **microorganisms**. Draw lines to match the cheese-making terms below with their definitions.

curds

culture

moulds

whey

fungi used to produce the veins in blue cheese

living microorganisms that ferment the milk

liquid produced after fermentation

solids produced from fermented milk

Q4 Complete the passage about **yoghurt making** by filling in the gaps using the words below.

| cooled | ferments | flavours | clots | heat-treated | lactic acid | bacteria |

To make yoghurt, milk is .... to kill off bacteria, then ....

Next, a starter culture of .... is added which .... the lactose

sugar into .... The milk then .... and forms yoghurt.

.... such as fruit are then added.

Using Yeast

Q1 Label the diagram of the **yeast cell** below.

b) ....

c) ....

a) ....

d) ....

e) ....

Q2 Circle the correct words to complete the sentences about yeast below.

a) Yeast is a **bacterium** / **fungus** / **virus**.

b) A yeast has a **single cell** / **many cells**.

c) Yeast can be used to make **bread** / **cheese** / **yoghurt**.

d) Yeast can respire **only aerobically** / **only anaerobically** / **both aerobically and anaerobically**.

e) Yeast is used to make a loaf of bread **lighter** / **heavier**.

Q3 Complete the passage by filling in the gaps using the words below.

ethanol	glucose	less	more	oxygen	water	carbon dioxide

Both aerobic and anaerobic respiration in yeast use ....

Anaerobic respiration is different from aerobic respiration as it doesn't need

............................, and it releases .... energy. Aerobic respiration

produces .... and ...., and releases ....

energy. Anaerobic respiration produces .... and carbon dioxide.

Q4 Below is a list of some of the stages involved in **beer making**.

- ☐ Barley grains are heated and dried.
- ☐ Barley grains are soaked in water and germinated.
- ☐ Hops are added.
- ☐ Malted grains are mashed with water.
- ☐ Yeast is added.

Lovely frothy beer.
Comes complete with
realistic disembodied hand.

a) Number these stages 1 to 5, where 1 is the first stage and 5 is the last.

b) Explain the purpose of adding the following:

i) hops ....

ii) yeast ....

c) State the important chemical changes that take place when:

i) the grains are germinating ....

ii) the yeast is fermenting ....

Biology 3(ii) — Microorganisms

<u>Using Yeast</u>

Q5   Beer production can go wrong unless the process is carefully controlled.
Draw lines to match each of the problems below with its possible cause.

fermentation doesn't start   barley grains are dead

fermentation stops too soon   fermentation vessel not clean

malt is not produced   temperature in fermenter gets too high

the beer goes sour   too many hops added

the beer is too bitter   yeast culture is dead

Q6   The graph below shows the results of an experiment on the **fermentation** of yeast.
The rate of **carbon dioxide** production was measured at different **temperatures**.

a)   What was the rate of carbon
dioxide production at 30 °C?

....

b)   What is the difference between the rate
of carbon dioxide production at 30 °C
and at 20 °C?

....

c)   i)   Describe the effect of increasing the temperature on the rate
of carbon dioxide production between 0 °C and 30 °C.

....

ii)   Suggest why this happens.

....

d)   Explain why the rate of carbon dioxide production at 60 °C is 0 cm³ per minute.

....

e)   During the experiment, all the conditions apart from temperature were kept constant.

i)   State **three** variables that would have been kept constant.

1. ....   2. ....   3. ....

ii)   Explain why it was important to keep these conditions constant.

....

f)   After obtaining these results, the experimenter repeated the whole experiment again.
Why did she do this?

....

Microorganisms in Industry

Q1 The diagram below shows a **fermenter** that can be used for producing **mycoprotein**.

a) Explain the purpose of each of the following:

i) the water jacket

....

ii) the air supply

....

iii) the paddles

....

b) Before fermentation begins, the fermenter is usually filled with hot steam, and then cooled. Why is this done?

....

c) Explain why this design of fermenter is probably not suitable for producing **wine**.

....

....

You want to produce ethanol when you're making wine.

Q2 A fermenter was used to produce **penicillin**. The graph below shows how the concentrations of nutrients and of penicillin changed over time.

a) When did the concentration of penicillin begin to increase the fastest?

....

b) Suggest reasons for each of the following:

i) The nutrient concentration falls slowly at first, and then more quickly.

....

....

ii) The penicillin concentration does not increase above 12 units.

....

....

c) During penicillin production, nutrients are **not** continually added to the fermenter. Why is this?

....

....

Fuels from Microorganisms

Q1   In the sentences below, circle the correct word.

a)   Fermentation is a form of **digestion** / **respiration**.

b)   Fermentation is **aerobic** / **anaerobic**.

c)   Fermentation by yeast produces **ethanol** / **methane**.

d)   Gasohol is a mixture of alcohol and **methane** / **petrol**.

Q2   Use the words below to fill in the gaps and complete the passage about **biogas**.

batch	generator	fermented	heating	turbine	waste

Biogas can be made in a container called a ...., either by continuous

production or by .... production. It is made from plant and animal

.... which is .... by microorganisms. Biogas could be used

for ...., or even to power a .... for making electricity.

Q3   Below are some stages in the making of **gasohol**.

☐ The product is mixed with petrol.
☐ Carbohydrase is added.
☐ Starch is extracted from a plant.
☐ The mixture is distilled.
☐ Yeast is added.

a)   Number these stages 1 to 5, where 1 is the first stage and 5 is the last.

b)   Explain the purpose of each of these stages:

i)   mixing the product with petrol 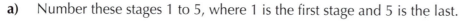 ....

ii) adding the carbohydrase   ....

iii) distilling the mixture   ....

iv) adding the yeast   ....

Q4   Below are some fairly straightforward questions about **biogas**. Great.

a)   Name the main components of biogas. ....

b)   Name **two** materials that might be used as food for the microorganisms used in producing biogas.

    ....

c)   Suggest an environmental advantage of using biogas (instead of natural gas) to heat a home

    ....

Fuels from Microorganisms

Q5 Fill in the blanks in the paragraph below using the words provided.

bacteria   carbon dioxide   methane   plants   environment

Biogas consists mainly of ...., which can be produced by ....

fermenting waste material. When biogas is burnt, it releases .... into the

atmosphere. This is not as damaging to the .... as burning fossil fuels, as it's

only returning carbon that was recently taken in by .... during photosynthesis.

Q6 Kapilisha did an experiment to produce **biogas** in the laboratory. After setting up the experiment, she left the apparatus in a warm place for five weeks. The diagram below shows her apparatus.

a) Describe the process that's going on inside the plastic bottle.

....

....

b) Why was the biomass mixed with distilled water, not tap water?

....

....

c) If biogas was produced, what change would be visible after a few weeks?

....

d) Explain why the bottle was left in a **warm** place during the five weeks.

....

Q7 Professor Wiggins did an experiment to find the best **temperature** for **biogas production**. The graph below shows what she found.

a) What is the best temperature for biogas production?

....

b) Professor Wiggins decided to set up her biogas generator at a temperature **slightly below** the best temperature. Suggest a reason for this.

....

....

c) Suggest **two** variables apart from temperature that might also affect the rate of biogas production.

....

....

d) Sewage can be used for biogas production, but it is important that the sewage contains as few chemical toxins as possible. Explain why this is important.

....

Fuels from Microorganisms

Q8 Biogas may be produced in a **batch** or **continuous** generator from waste materials, e.g. animal waste. Circle the correct words below to describe how a batch and continuous generator differ.

a) In a **batch** / **continuous** generator, waste is usually loaded manually.

b) A **batch** / **continuous** generator is the best choice for large-scale production.

c) In a continuous generator, waste is added **at intervals** / **all the time**.

d) In a **batch** / **continuous** generator, biogas is produced at a steady rate.

Q9 In a village in South America, a **biogas generator** was built.

a) Suggest reasons for the following features of the design:

  i) The generator was built some distance away from houses in the village.

  ....

  ii) The generator was built close to fields where animals were grazing.

  ....

  iii) The generator was covered with insulating material.

  ....

b) Describe **two** possible advantages for the villagers in having a biogas generator like this.

  ....

  ....

Q10 The diagram below shows a **biogas generator system**.

a) The energy in biogas originally came from the **Sun**. Explain how.

  ....

  ....

b) How can biogas power **electrical appliances**?

  ....

c) Biogas is sometimes described as being '**carbon neutral**'.

  i) Explain why biogas is carbon neutral.

  ....

  ii) Name **one** other type of fuel which is **not** carbon neutral.

  ....

  iii) Name **two other** reasons why biogas is less damaging to the environment than many fuels.

  ....

  ....

Using Microorganisms Safely

Q1 Draw lines to match each of the following terms with their meanings.

contamination   killing all microorganisms

growth medium   the presence of unwanted microorganisms or substances

inoculating loop   used for transferring microorganisms into a culture

sterilisation   a material containing nutrients for the growth of a microorganism

Q2 **Microorganisms** can be **grown** in the laboratory on a Petri dish.

a) List **two** nutrients that might be added to a Petri dish to help microorganisms grow.

....

b) Explain why:

i) A lid should be kept on the Petri dish before and after the microorganisms are added.

....

ii) The microorganisms should be transferred using an inoculating loop which has been passed through a flame.

....

iii) After going through the flame, the inoculating loop must be cooled before it's used to pick up the microorganisms.

....

iv) The experimenter should wash their hands carefully before the start of the experiment.

....

Q3 A scientist grew some **bacteria** on a nutrient medium in two Petri dishes. He kept the two dishes at different temperatures, 25 °C and 37 °C. The graph shows the **rates of growth** of the bacteria.

a) Compare the growth of the bacteria at the two temperatures:

i) At which temperature did the bacteria grow faster?

....

ii) Give **one** reason why they grew faster at this temperature.

....

iii) What happened to the bacterial colony growing at 37 °C after four days? Why did this happen?

....

....

b) Suggest why the scientist chose 37 °C as one of the temperatures in his experiment.

....

c) Explain why Petri dishes are usually incubated at 25 °C in school experiments.

....

Mixed Questions — Biology 3(ii)

Q1   **Yoghurt** is made using bacteria.

a)   Explain why:

i)   The milk is heated to 85 °C before the process starts.

....

ii)   A small amount of 'live' yoghurt is added to the milk.

....

iii)   The mixture is kept at 45 °C for a few hours.

....

b)   Name **one** other food that is also made using bacteria. ....

Q2   The diagram below shows an experiment to demonstrate fermentation by **yeast**.

a)   At the start, **oxygen** is present in the air above the yeast.

i)   What type of respiration will the yeast use?

....

ii)   What is the advantage of this for the yeast?

....

iii)   Explain what changes you would expect to see in the limewater.

....

b)   Later, the yeast begin to respire differently. Why does this change happen?

....

c)   After a while, the yeast die and sink to the bottom of the boiling tube. Suggest **two** reasons why.

....

....

Q3   Home wine makers use an **airlock** like the one shown.
Bubbles of gas can escape out of the container, but air cannot get in.

a)   Why do wine makers use airlocks?

....

b)   Name **two** ingredients that you will need if you want to make wine at home.

1. ....   2. ....

Biology 3(ii) — Microorganisms

Mixed Questions — Biology 3(ii)

Q4 Draw lines to match each of the terms below with its correct description.

fermenter

Fusarium

mycoprotein

penicillin

Penicillium

an antibiotic

a container in which microorganisms can be grown

a food produced by fermentation

an organism used for growing food

an organism used for producing a drug

Q5 The table below summarises two different ways in which **yeast** can release energy. Complete the table, choosing words from the following list.

glucose   oxygen   carbon dioxide   ethanol   water

process	aerobic respiration	fermentation
reactants		
products		

Q6 Doctor Large works for a biotechnology company. He was asked to do an experiment to find the best temperature for the growth of a **fungus**.

a) Explain the reasons behind the following features of his experiment:

i) All of the tests were carried out at a pH of 7.

....

ii) He tested each temperature twice.

....

b) What should he measure, at the end of each test, to find out how well the fungus has grown?

....

c) Doctor Large found that the best temperature for fungus growth was 25 °C. Suggest why:

i) a lower temperature was not as good for fungus growth.

....

ii) a higher temperature was not as good for fungus growth.

....

Mixed Questions — Biology 3(ii)

Q7   Circle the correct words in each sentence below.

a)   Fermentation is a form of **digestion** / **respiration**.

b)   Fermentation is **aerobic** / **anaerobic**.

c)   Fermentation by yeast produces **ethanol** / **methane**.

d)   Gasohol is a mixture of alcohol and **methane** / **petrol**.

Q8   **Biogas** is a fuel that can be made easily from plant and animal waste.

a)   Explain the difference between **continuous** and **batch** biogas generators.

....

....

....

b)   State **two** reasons why biogas is a 'greener' alternative to fossil fuels.

....

....

Q9   Explain what each of the following are:

a)   **agar** ....

b)   **culture medium** ....

c)   **pathogen** ....

Q10   At 7 am, John made a chicken sandwich, then wrapped it up and put it in the inside pocket of his jacket. In this warm place, **bacteria** can divide and double their numbers every 30 minutes.

a)   If the sandwich picked up 100 bacteria from John's hands at 7 am, how many bacteria might it contain by the time he eats the sandwich at 11 am? Show your working.

....

....

b)   Suggest **two** things that John could have done to reduce the growth of bacteria on his sandwich.

....

....

c)   Explain why it would not be a good idea for John to keep his sandwich and eat it the next day.

....